Ashbourne: its history and treasures

From the Bronze Age to the digital age

by Adrian Henstock

First published in 2017

by The Ashbourne Treasures Group

ISBN 0954146433

History text by Adrian Henstock
Exhibits text by Geof Cole and John Titterton
Graphic design and picture editing by Philip Gregory
Photography by members of Ashbourne Camera Club, John Robey, Peter Walker and Lindsay Trevarthen

Contents

FOREWORD

Derbyshire is fortunate in having a number of distinctive market towns each with its own unique character. Ashbourne is one of these and five local organisations have come together to mount a celebration of the town's history in the Ashbourne Treasures exhibition. This community project, supported by the Heritage Lottery Fund, includes, apart from the exhibition, a series of lectures, special church services, a new heritage walk, updating the town's fingerposts and more.

Amongst the more than 40 objects on display in the three-month exhibition are a number rarely seen, either because they are in museums or held privately. I am delighted that it will be possible to view the original seal of Queen Elizabeth's Grammar School, presently housed in the British Museum, together with the original beautifully illuminated Royal Charter, also from 1585, normally stored in the Derbyshire Record Office. Details and photographs of all the Treasures can be found in this book, which combines the catalogue within the history of the town, written by local historian Adrian Henstock.

Congratulations to the Ashbourne Treasures Group for bringing this community initiative to fruition and whether you are local or a visitor to the town, this book will help you appreciate what a wonderful place Ashbourne is.

William Tucker
HM Lord Lieutenant of Derbyshire

INTRODUCTION

A painting by Henry Lark Pratt of Ashbourne provides the viewer with a panoramic view, dominated by the needle-thin spire of St Oswald's Church, rising 212 feet into the sky. The artist's viewpoint is from the cliff that rises to the south side of the town, looking towards the desolation of the Peak, and his scene records the new train arriving in the town. Alas, the trains have gone, and Ashbourne's Church Street groans to the sound of lorries passing from Derby to Buxton, dropping down one hill before grinding up the other side.

In the middle is the Henmore Brook, a tributary of the anglers' paradise, the River Dove, whose valley provides a route from the south, through lush farms, narrow lanes hemmed in with high hedges and towering broadleaf trees. Approach from this direction and the curious pyramid of Thorpe Cloud, guardian of Dovedale, will arrest the traveller's eye. The brook plays a legendary role in Ashbourne's famous Shrovetide football match. The icy February water and the associated winter mud all add to the centuries-old, two-day spectacle.

With a little imagination, it is easy to time travel in Ashbourne. Stepping down Church Street, one of the finest streets in Derbyshire, is to walk back to 1585 when the original Grammar School building was founded. Amongst Ashbourne's greatest treasures are its commitment to the education of its children (latterly girls as well as boys), and materially, the charter itself of the school, illuminated with the miniature of Queen Elizabeth I, attributed to Nicholas Hilliard. Along the street, the buildings retain their individual period architecture, handsome stone properties, alongside timber (original and later additions) frontages, and red brick houses, marking this as a prosperous Midland town. Tourists who now arrive in their own cars, would have arrived in horse-drawn coaches, pulling up at one of the many inns, before setting out to explore the glories of Dovedale and venturing into the 'howling wilderness' to find the Wonders of the Peak, or continuing northwards all the way to Carlisle (following in the retreating footsteps of Bonnie Prince Charlie). An industrious town too, despite its reputation for having so many public houses, where people made gloves and clocks, and farmers sold their produce.

Step into the church to see the esteem in which the people considered their place within the community, with its magnificent 17th century church plate, and rich monuments, most famously Thomas Bank's memorial to Penelope Boothby. This marble sculpture of childish innocence is said to have moved Queen Charlotte to tears. But look around, and medieval England comes to life in the sculptured images of the Cokaynes who lived at the time of the Wars of the Roses. This building has been improved and altered over the centuries, but was dedicated in 1220 when Henry III ruled England, and it is likely built on Saxon and Viking spiritual foundations.

Indeed, this gateway town must have seen many comings and goings even before this. Late in the Roman occupation, sometime after 293 AD, someone lost two gold coins minted for the renegade emperor Carausius near the town - or were they buried? Go slightly north, and the Romans settled in the area now flooded by Carsington Reservoir, farming and supervising the mining and production of lead. Meanwhile, in Dovedale in about 70 AD, another purse was lost by a member of the Corieltavi tribe, this time of British, not Roman, coin. Small incidences; time does not allow us to keep all the detritus of all the people yet these scraps let us glimpse a time when the place now called Ashbourne was busy with many people trading, farming, telling stories and gossiping.

My first memory of Ashbourne was the rich, sweet smell of milk being condensed. That factory is now gone, its site redeveloped. Then, at Christmas when the main street is dressed with so many lights that traveller's spirit, accustomed to the dark, are raised with joy; in the summer when the copious bunting shakes and flutters in the wind-filled sky. This market town projects a confidence in its past; and, with innovative businesses, a high street served by an array of independent stores, a spacious new library and its historic market, there is optimism too for its future.

Ros Westwood
Derbyshire Museums Manager

ASHBOURNE: ITS HISTORY AND TREASURES
From the Bronze Age to the digital age
with a catalogue of treasures
by Adrian Henstock

This account does not attempt to be a comprehensive narrative history of Ashbourne but a chronological series of themes and topics designed to set the objects displayed in the Ashbourne Treasures exhibition of 2017 into their historical context. It incorporates previously unpublished or less accessible research and details of recent archaeological discoveries, etc.

References to individual Treasures appear in their respective chronological sequence.
Each one is described and illustrated on separate coloured pages.

Introduction

Ashbourne is an historic Derbyshire market town thirteen miles north west of Derby and a mile to the east of the River Dove – the boundary between Derbyshire and Staffordshire – at the junction between the East and the West Midlands. The town stands in the valley of the small tributary River Henmore at the meeting point of six main roads, all of them the descendants of turnpike roads of the 1700s or 1800s but many of much older origin. One of the principal historical routes from London to Manchester and the north-west passed through the town and crossed the Dove by the mediaeval Hanging Bridge.

Ashbourne is built predominantly of red brick and as such is a typical Midland market town, but its scattered stone buildings are a reminder of its role in the life of the Peak District immediately to the north; indeed up to the 1700s it was often known as Ashbourne-in-the-Peak. The dramatic limestone hills of Thorpe Cloud and Bunster – twin bastions of the entrance to the Dovedale gorge – are only four miles away surrounded by drystone wall country. Along with the Weaver Hills in the Staffordshire Moorlands to the west these form the end of the Pennine chain which reaches down the backbone of England. Yet at a similar distance to the south the undulating hedgerow country might be part of Leicestershire or Warwickshire.

The northern villages such as Tissington and Thorpe are constructed of white limestone but the western villages of Mayfield, Stanton, Ellastone are of superior brown-red sandstone. This stone was notably also used for two of Ashbourne's most historic buildings – the mediaeval parish church and the Elizabethan Old Grammar School. To the east and south poorer pebbly and sandy sandstones are unsuitable for building and give way to a marlstone plateau which gradually slopes away to the more fertile arable soils of the lower Dove valley.

For over eight hundred years Ashbourne provided markets where the products of these two contrasting landscapes could be interchanged – cattle, sheep, wool, lead and lime from the uplands in return for horses, corn, and timber – a town where craftsmen could work and merchants sell their goods.

Prehistoric period (*pre*-c.50 AD)

The history of man in the Ashbourne area can be traced back to the Neolithic era, when the limestone plateau to the north was settled by primitive farmers whose 'tumuli' or burial mounds – locally called 'lows' - are still to be found in considerable numbers alongside spectacular monuments such as the Arbor Low 'henge' or stone circle near Hartington.

In the immediate area of the town round barrows dating from the Bronze Age are mostly found in the Dovedale hills to the north, although with a significant group of at least six alongside the Wyaston road to the south and another line on the ridge behind Mayfield to the west. Three more on a now lost site above Mapleton were excavated by Samuel Carrington in 1849. There was also a barrow at the top of the Old Hill and another at the summit of the town's Buxton Road – an area historically known as Low Top. Not far along the ridge from here – near Ashley – a Bronze Age metal axe head was discovered in 2006 which may have come from a barrow.
[Treasure no L1: Bronze axe head]

An unusually complex multi-period group of barrows is at Wigber Low in Kniveton parish on a prominent hill overlooking the Parwich valley. In the Neolithic period it appears to have been used as a periodic camp revealed by finds of flint flakes and tools along with

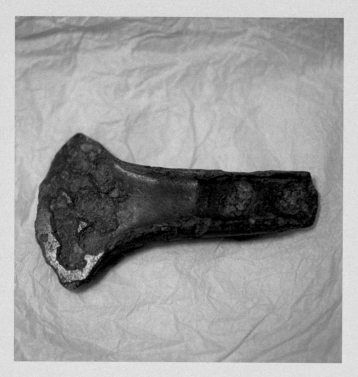

L1

Bronze axe head

c.1600 BC
Found near Ashbourne in 2006
On loan from Mr M Gadsby

This flanged axe head is from the Arreton industrial phase of the Bronze Age – around 3,700 to around 3,500 years ago - and represents a significant development in metal tools.

Axe heads were mounted through a wooden shaft, and the first metal axe heads were flat, replicating earlier stone versions. The use of flanges ensured that the axe head fitted more securely into the handle. The head with its flanges would have been cast in one piece.

Such axes were expensive and time consuming to make and would have been a prized possession. It may have been buried with its owner, or simply lost.

imported stone hand axes. The site was later used an ex-carnation platform where at least twenty-one bodies were exposed to natural animal predators. Later burials were made on the same site – one as late as the post-Roman Anglian period.

A recent discovery is the *Dovedale Hoard* of twenty-six gold and silver coins dating from the late Iron Age found in Reynard's Kitchen cave in 2014. All the coins predate the Roman invasion of Britain. While the bulk are attributed to the Iron Age Corieltavi tribe who lived in the East Midland lowlands at least three are of Roman origin – the first instance of coins from these two civilizations found buried together. Cave hoards are usually associated with hasty burials of personal wealth – either in times of war or unsettled political conditions – or else they represent stolen property never recovered.

Roman period (c.50 – c.450 AD)

The Roman conquest of Britain commenced in 43 AD and by the late 70s most of modern Derbyshire had been subdued. The Peak District was attractive for its mineral deposits, especially of lead ore. The headquarters of lead production was called *Lutudarum* and appears to have been in the Matlock or Carsington areas, where several settlements of Romano-British date have been excavated. Nearer Ashbourne evidence of a similar settlement, including 'Celtic' fields, has been identified on the slopes of Thorpe Cloud in Dovedale.

The local area was very quickly surrounded by a triangle of Roman military roads. The most important led from Little Chester (*Derventio*) near Derby north-westwards to the Roman spa at Buxton (*Aquae Armetiae*), but its course is lost south of Carsington. A road ran east-west from Little Chester along Long Lane some five miles south of Ashbourne to a military fort sited at the crossing of the River Dove at Rocester. From there it continued towards Chester, being joined near Blythe Bridge by another possible road running south from Buxton and Leek.

A suspected Roman road connecting Rocester with Chesterfield via Ashbourne and Cromford has been postulated, but although the route may have been in use at this period its identification with a documented mediaeval highway called the 'Hereward Street' cannot be substantiated.

However numerous pre-existing local trackways must have been created by the native Britons, many of which were used by the Romans for non-military purposes. Circumstantial topographical and archaeological evidence suggests that a long-distance trackway linked the Trent valley near Burton-on-Trent with Tutbury and Ashbourne, continuing via Thorpe towards Hartington and the Peak. If so its likely route may have been via the Old Hill and Compton, as there are no less than four references in documents dated between 1258 and 1275 to *Campedene stret(e)*; the word 'street' means a paved way, often a Roman road, and all other references to town streets in the modern sense appear much later.

It may be significant that two Roman ingots (the '*Yeaveley pigs-of lead'*) were found in 1975 by the roadside some four miles south of Ashbourne near Yeaveley village; the site is exactly on the route of this postulated trackway and a mile north of the Little Chester to Rocester road. They both bear a Latin inscription referring to *Lutudarum* as seen on twenty-five other ingots found within the county and elsewhere. One can speculate that they may have been stolen from a cart travelling west from Derby towards Rocester and brought up the track for concealment, or conversely were being carted direct from the Carsington area via Ashbourne to Burton for onward transport either along the Trent or south along Rykneld Street.

Another lead 'pig' or ingot, presumed to date from the Roman or immediate post-Roman period, was found at Ilam in 2007. It is rectangular in shape with various crude and irregular markings but bears no inscription.

The Staffordshire Moorlands Pan

A remarkable Roman artefact was found in 2003. It is now known as the *Staffordshire Moorlands Pan* and is of international importance. Although in form a domestic metal pan (lacking its handle) it is decorated with flamboyant free-flowing Celtic-style decoration inlaid with coloured enamels. It bears a Latin inscription listing several forts along Hadrian's Wall and is customised with the name of its owner – a man called 'Draco'. It is the best example of only three such pans found in Britain and France. Remarkably archaeologists have pronounced them to be souvenirs acquired by veteran soldiers who had served on the Wall. It dates from the end of the 1st century AD *(see illustration)*

The question is how did it reach its find spot over a hundred miles south of the wall? It was found on the northern slopes of the Manifold valley not far from the site of later lead mines near Wetton; these may possibly have been worked in Roman times, so could the owner have been employed guarding the mines adjacent to a suspected nearby Romano-British village? A more plausible explanation is that as such pans are found in relation to water and spas they may have played a part in ritual devotions to the gods.

It is significant that the Manifold – having run several miles underground in summer – reappears from a 'boil hole' near Ilam church. In post-Roman times Ilam was a place of pilgrimage associated with the shrine and holy well of the local saint Bertelin/Bertram and the site could have served a similar purpose for the Roman gods?

Staffordshire Moorlands Pan

The Potteries Museum & Art Gallery, Stoke-on-Trent

Jointly acquired by the British Museum,
the Potteries Museum & Art Gallery, Stoke-on-Trent, and the Tullie House Museum and Art Gallery, Carlisle

The Ashbourne Hoard

Two extremely rare Roman gold coins or 'aureus', now known as the *Ashbourne Hoard,* were found in Kniveton parish overlooking the valley of the Bentley Brook in 2007. They date from the period of the Roman emperor Carausius (AD 286-93) who declared himself emperor of a breakaway 'empire' covering Northern Gaul and Britain. Only twenty-three coins from his reign have ever been found. One of the finds was struck at the London mint, the other at Rouen, and they imply the presence in the area of a high-status Roman official *(see illustration)*.

Carausius coin
Derby Museums

Anglian & Mercian period (c.500 – 1066)

Little is known about the period after the withdrawal of the Roman legions between c.350 and c.450 AD, which left the country open to invasions by Germanic invaders from the Angle peninsular in the 500s and the 600s. They began to settle in East Anglia and then the East Midlands, approaching via the Trent Valley. They were probably late in reaching the Dove valley, although an Anglian cremation grave from the 500s has apparently been identified at Musden near Ilam.

The Anglian settlements

Place names provide a useful indication of the nature of Anglian settlements. Historians now believe that the earliest names are those which are simply topographical descriptions of the local landscape. These include river names such as Bradbourne – the 'broad burn or stream' and Ashbourne itself – 'ash tree burn'. Other examples are names ending in *'feld'* – referring to extensive open pastures in woodland as at Alstonefield, and *'ofer'* meaning a bank on the edge of a ridge as at Okeover – 'oak tree bank'.

A high proportion of modern village names are believed to date from the late 700s onwards. Many have the common ending *'ton'* meaning a farm or settlement, often prefixed by the name of the leader of the Anglian band or family who founded it, for example Osmaston was originally 'Osmund's farm'. He and three other leaders named Eadwulf, Wig(e)hard and Snell became close neighbours after they had established four adjoining villages; these we now know as Osmaston, Edlaston, Wyaston and Snelston. Kniveton is unusual in that it was named after a woman called Cengifu.

The settlers also began the clearance of the well-wooded land in the south of the town which their predecessors had shunned. Here is a cluster of adjacent names ending in *'ley'* - meaning woodland cleared for farming – e.g. Cub*ley*, Yeave*ley*, Yelders*ley*, Shir*ley* and Rods*ley*; the first three were settled by men named Cubba, Geofa and Geldhere respectively. Woodland is also indicated by oak trees at Okeover, maples at Mapleton, and ash trees at Ashbourne.

Immediately to the east was an undulating landscape dissected by steep-sided wooded valleys (locally called dumbles) which appears to have been cleared randomly over the centuries, leaving a mixture of enclosures and open patches of common pasture called 'greens'. The area was called Under-wood and included the large open space still surviving in reduced form as Ashbourne Green.

The Peak Dwellers

There is limited but suggestive documentary evidence that by the 600s the whole of what is now north and west Derbyshire became a separate tribal region of the native Britons but ruled by an Anglian king or chieftain. The inhabitants were known as the *'Pecsaete'* or 'Peak dwellers' and grave sites show that members of their aristocracy lived close to Ashbourne, especially on the limestone plateau east of the Dovedale gorge. Here several burials from the 600s have been excavated which contained high status weaponry, jewellery and other objects. Near Tissington a silver-mounted sword and shield boss was found at Boar's Low and a female grave at Stand Low contained a glass bead necklace, a circular bronze thread-box with a serpent's head handle, and a silver needle.

The most spectacular find was the well-known Benty Grange helmet excavated near Hartington which may have belonged to their chieftain. The helmet is constructed from an iron frame infilled with horn secured by silver rivets and with a silver cross over the nose guard; it is crowned by a bronze figure of a wild boar ornamented with silver studs and garnet 'eyes'. This combination of pagan and Christian symbols indicates that its owner was backing both religious beliefs. Two silver crosses and enamel ornaments were associated with the same burial.

Occasional Anglian burials have been found to the south of Ashbourne. A female burial site at Wyaston contained a necklace made up of five amber beads mixed with twenty-two variegated white, red, yellow and blue ceramic beads, a silver wire ring with an ornamental knot, and fragmentary silver earrings.

The extent of the Pecsaetan territory is a subject of debate, although it is possible that at some period its southern boundary was in the vicinity of the Henmore valley. During the late 600s it must have been absorbed by King Offa into his expanding kingdom of Mercia – whose heartlands were around Repton, Tamworth and Lichfield – although a royal land charter of 963 still describes Ballidon as being *'in the district of the Pecsaetan'*. The areas occupied by the modern counties of Staffordshire, Derbyshire and Nottinghamshire became buffer states against the Northumbrians from the north.

Christianity began to be adopted in Mercia in the late 600s and 700s and the Ashbourne area became part of a newly created Mercian diocese based at Lichfield. This also led to the emergence of a flourishing school of Anglian/Mercian sculpture in the late 700s and early 800s which produced several preaching crosses with elaborate twisted vine scrolls and stylised figures, the best example being at Bradbourne.

Following the re-conquest and the ultimate unification of all the country (surprisingly named 'Angle-land' – England) under a single Anglo-Saxon king numerous administrative changes took place. Shires came into existence for the first time, defined as areas subject to major boroughs such as Derby and Nottingham. These were subdivided into districts called by the Danish word 'wapentakes' (where voting was conducted by the flourishing of weapons). Domesday Book of 1086 is the first document to record their names.

Ashbourne was then at the very south-western tip of 'Hamelstan' Wapentake, divided from Appletree Wapentake by the River Henmore. The meeting place of its council is believed to have been at Hamston Hill – a rocky outcrop overlooking Dovedale near Thorpe and close to the proposed ancient trackway mentioned above. Significantly 'Hamelstan' Wapentake covered the whole of the ancient territory of the Pecsaetan, but was later split into two – High Peak and Wirksworth Wapentakes (sometimes referred to as 'Wirksworth & Ashbourne'). The residents of Appletree Wapentake presumably met near to a prominent apple tree, possibly near Sutton-on-the Hill.

Anglo-Saxon crosses and minster churches

It is impossible to tell when a religious settlement was first established at Ashbourne but it could have been as early as the 600s in view of the church's dedication to King Oswald of Northumbria, who was revered as a saint following his death in battle in 642. Shortly after this the king of Mercia invited priests from Lindisfarne to convert Mercia, including St Chad who settled at Lichfield.

Another theory is that such a settlement followed the Christian reconversion of the Danelaw in the early 900s when the bones of St Oswald are known to have been dispersed. Whatever the date was it is highly probable that one or more of his bones was given to Ashbourne's original church to be venerated as a relic, which was a frequent occurrence. A 'reliquary' to house such relics was discovered behind the high altar of the present church during Victorian restorations, along with the section of a preaching cross shaft now preserved in the north transept. **[Treasure no C1: Anglo-Saxon cross shaft]**

The Vikings and the Danelaw

The political situation changed dramatically at the end of the 800s. Viking raiders from Denmark made several incursions into the East Midlands, culminating in an invasion by a 'Great Army' which sailed up the River Trent in 874. They spent the winter in a fortification built at Repton and drove the king of Mercia into exile. This event was no doubt the reason for the burial of the 'Beeston Tor hoard', found in a cave in the Manifold Valley in 1924, which included brooches and coins dating from precisely that period. Shortly afterwards a few Vikings began to settle in the area, as the Anglo-Saxon Chronicle recorded that some *'proceeded to plough and support themselves'*.

Although there is less evidence of Danish influence on place names in the Ashbourne area compared to the east of the region, there are a few examples, such as the word 'dale' for a valley as in Dovedale. The names of Stur*ston* and Ros*ton* both bear the Anglian suffix *'ton'* but are prefixed by Viking personal names of Styrr and Hrosskell respectively, suggesting that these men may have forcibly taken over existing farms. In addition some later mediaeval references to the 'ash burn' – the river from which the town took its name – are written in the Scandinavian form as the 'ask beck'. The name Thorpe is Danish for an outlying or secondary settlement, but as the word was soon

C1
Anglo-Saxon cross shaft

c.920
Sandstone
St Oswald's Church

This is the oldest artefact in St Oswald's Church. In 1886, there was a record of two fragments, but one is now missing. A churchyard cross is shown on the map of 1547 and this cross shaft may be a remnant.

All four sides on the cross show an interlaced pattern, which was common in this area but the irregularity of the interfaces is unusual. One of the narrow faces has a two-strand interlaced pattern in a style known as the Stafford Knot, which occurs throughout Staffordshire and Derbyshire. The hind legs of an animal can be seen on one of the broad sides of the shaft. Crosses with animal forms are often found in the valley of the River Trent and its tributaries such as the Dove.

The Ashbourne cross is likely to be a memorial commemorating the re-conquest of this part of the Kingdom of Mercia from the Danes in the early 900s.

adopted by the English as well this may not be significant.

The Viking invasion was ultimately successful and the Anglian borough of Northworthy was given the Viking name of Deoraby (Derby) – the 'deer farm'. The whole of the East Midlands passed under Danish rule and law and became known as the Danelaw. Its western boundary is the subject of debate but Staffordshire almost certainly remained part of Mercia. If so it would mean that the River Dove – and Ashbourne – became frontier territory.

Two villages some five miles apart on the eastern (Derbyshire) bank of the Dove to the south of the town – Norbury and Sudbury – bear names which mean the 'north-' and the 'south fortification', presumably in relation to a site in between. This must refer to the river crossing at Rocester carrying the Roman road (Long Lane) leading towards Derby from Mercia. It is tempting to speculate that the fortifications refer to temporary Danish defences erected to protect the three crossings?

An obvious occasion for such action would be during the wars of c.917–920 when the Danelaw was slowly reconquered by Æthelflæd – the formidable 'Lady of the Mercians' – in conjunction with her brother King Edward of Wessex. The Mercian armies recaptured Derby in 917 before advancing north through the Peak District, where they constructed a fortification near Bakewell in 920.

This, along with similar shafts at Ilam and the two at Norbury, all date from the 900s and 1000s and are products of a local Anglo-Danish sculptural school. Numerous smaller fragments are built into the fabric of Alstonefield church. In addition Ilam may well have been a place of pilgrimage associated with the shrine and holy well of the local Anglian Saint Bertelin or Bertram

What appears to be certain is that the settlement at Ashbourne was primarily religious. As with Wirksworth, Bakewell, and Hope it almost certainly served as a missionary centre or 'minster' – a mother church for a vast parish, funded by income from tithes and other offerings from surrounding villages in the Dove catchment area. Several villages such as Parwich and Thorpe later became independent parishes but many survived as outlying chapelries for centuries after. It is possible that Bradbourne was also an early minster centre which at some time in the late Anglian period may have been brought into Ashbourne's missionary orbit along with Brassington, Tissington and perhaps Hognaston and Kniveton.

Mediaeval period (1066 – c.1540)

The Norman Conquest and confiscation of Anglian estates

William, Duke of Normandy, launched an invasion of England in 1066 to claim the English throne and triumphed at the Battle of Hastings. He subsequently rewarded his Norman knights with vast grants of land confiscated from the previous Anglo–Saxon landowners. Twenty years later in 1086 he commissioned the *Domesday Book,* a remarkable taxation survey and valuation written in Latin of all the towns and villages throughout his recently acquired realm.

As with most places, Ashbourne appears for the first time in the written record – spelt by the Norman French speaking assessors as *Esseburne* but probably pronounced not much differently as today as '*esh-burn'*. It reveals that King Edward had continued to protect the old Mercian borders by bringing together a group of six extensive Peak district estates under direct royal control. Such estates were centred on villages but were now called 'manors' – administered from manor houses where their lords (owners) held their courts. Important manors often had subsidiary hamlets.

These estates were those of Ashbourne, Parwich, Wirksworth, Darley (Dale), Bakewell and Hope with all their dependent settlements, which together included most of the wapentakes of Wirksworth and High Peak. Ashbourne's dependencies included Offcote, Mapleton, (Fenny) Bentley, Thorpe, Broadlow Ash (now part of Thorpe) and – some distance away – Hognaston. Parwich manor accounted for Alsop with the adjacent hamlets of (Cold) Eaton, and Hanson (Grange). When all these estates had been taken into royal hands is not known. In 966 King Edgar had given away Parwich with its dependencies to one of his retainers, although by 1066 it had obviously returned into royal hands.

This whole group was now taken over by the new Norman King William. Across the Dove the king also took over Mayfield and Rocester, possibly to protect their bridging points, and smaller settlements in the Ilam and Alton areas. The remaining local manors were farmed out as rewards to his loyal knights and barons, the great majority to Henry de Ferrers

Domesday Book of 1086: Ashbourne's countryside

The Norman surveyors of Domesday Book were required to estimate the present value of each manor. The value of arable land was assessed in terms of the number of plough-teams of oxen which were employed both on the lord's own 'demesne' (home farm and land) and on the land farmed by the villagers. Some manors were described as 'waste' and of no value. Historians have long debated whether this term meant areas devastated by King William's brutal military campaigns or simply uncultivated pastureland. The latter seems far more likely in Derbyshire as all such places – including Ashbourne's and Parwich's dependent hamlets and the Hartington and Alstonefield areas – were situated in marginal hill country.

The surveyors also had to seek out retrospective valuations which had pertained at the end of the reign of the last Anglo-Saxon king, Edward the Confessor. It is obvious that the battles and political upheavals of the Conquest and its aftermath had taken their toll and all of some forty settlements within Ashbourne's hinterland recorded a fall in value since King Edward's time of something like a half to a third. For example Sturston had dropped from £2 to £1 and Norbury from £5 to £3.

The survey also enumerated the inhabitants on each estate. These were unfree peasants divided into two categories. The first was those *villagers* who worked land for themselves but were also obliged to work for the lord of the manor for two or three days per week. The second was *cottagers* or smallholders. The totals varied greatly between a single resident in Yeldersley to twenty-six in Norbury and Roston and twenty-eight in Rocester. In order to arrive at an approximation of the total population all these figures should be multiplied by about five to include their families.

Churches with priests were recorded at Ashbourne, Bradbourne, Shirley, Norbury, Cubley, and Sudbury, and a priest only at Mayfield. With the possible exception of Bradbourne most of these would have been wooden structures. Many other villages may have had churches but these were ignored if they had no tax implications. A surprising omission from the survey is Ilam, even though the hamlets of Musden and Stanshope do appear, especially in view of its probable venue as an ancient shrine.

Mills were particularly valuable as every tenant was obliged to use the lord's mill to grind his corn. They were recorded at Norbury, Ellastone, Rocester, Sudbury and Okeover, all on the Dove, at Sturston on the Henmore and another at Tissington, probably on the Bentley Brook; many of these sites would have continued in use into modern times.

Domesday Book of 1086: Ashbourne manor

As so often with Domesday Book it is difficult to interpret the cryptic entry for Ashbourne and to determine the exact meaning of the Latin terminology. **[Treasure no H1: Domesday Book]** It appears to show that, apart from the church property there were apparently no inhabitants at all on the lord's, i.e. royal, manor. Although there was 'land for three ploughs' the statement that '(it is) waste, but it pays 20 shillings' infers that the soil was uncultivated but perhaps still produced an income from livestock farming. It does record a population of eleven villagers and seventeen cottagers but these only relate to the six named outlying villages collectively.

What the Ashbourne entry does reveal is that there was a church and a priest with land for one plough, and he had two villagers and two cottagers who between them had half a plough. This obviously relates to the church's status as a 'minster' or mission station serving the surrounding countryside. It had been endowed – presumably by a former king or aristocratic Anglian landowner – with a quantity of land to provide the priest with a 'living' whilst he concentrated on the cure of souls. This would have to be augmented by the 'tithes' (one-tenth of each farmer's produce from corn or livestock) and other offerings from his parish. His four tenants ploughed their own land as well as some of his, presumably sharing a plough-team of oxen. He had one plough of his own, assisted by a 'man' who probably worked on the farm but who paid 16 pence for some other service.

The priest obviously held what historians call a 'rectory manor' i.e. a pseudo-manorial estate owned by the parish rector separate from the royal (later baronial) manor of Ashbourne. It is a reminder that in the Middle Ages some of the largest landowners were ecclesiastical organisations, such as monasteries, cathedrals and colleges. The entry confirms that the old Anglian church settlement within its large parish still existed as an independent unit. It will be referred to hereafter as the church manor.

The manor of Ashbourne did not include Compton and the area south of the Henmore, which in 1086 fell within Clifton and Sturston manors respectively. Clifton possessed land for four ploughs and a population of thirteen. Ironically Sturston (with its adjacent lost hamlet of Fenton – the 'fenny farm') was the largest of the three manors, having six ploughs and the surprisingly high number of twenty-one inhabitants.

H1
Domesday Book

1086

Parchment

The National Archives

The first recorded reference to Ashbourne occurs in the Domesday Book of 1086, which was the manuscript record of a 'great survey' ordered by William the Conqueror. The main aims of the survey were to find out who owned the land and what income was due to the king. It was the product of a highly efficient English administration, and was written in an abbreviated form of medieval Latin.

The settlement, then known as Esseburne, was a hamlet with a church and a resident priest. Ashbourne was likely to be primarily a religious centre with a 'minster' or mother parish church for neighbouring villages.

The appropriation of the Ashbourne church manor by Lincoln Cathedral

The 1000s and 1100s saw the construction of great Norman cathedrals throughout the country, and to help finance them, Norman kings often granted them the income from wealthy parishes. In this manner Ashbourne rectory and its income was granted by King William (Rufus) II to the newly-consecrated Lincoln Cathedral in 1093. By the same grant Lincoln also received the rectories of Chesterfield, Mansfield and elsewhere together with all their dependent chapels. Wirksworth was added later, so the Dean of Lincoln held a string of wealthy parishes conveniently situated in topographical order for the ease of collecting tithes.

In c.1200 the Dean 'appropriated' Ashbourne rectory, i.e. he effectively became the parish rector and installed a vicar ('deputy') to carry out the services. Only half the income from tithes was allocated to the vicar and the rest went to the dean. Every time a new vicar was subsequently appointed the dean's proportion of the income was increased, and by 1290 it was arranged that he would receive the 'great tithes' (i.e. the most valuable) and the vicar the 'lesser tithes'. By way of partial compensation he gave a plot of land for the erection of a vicarage immediately south of the church *'bounded on the one side by the road leading from the churchyard to the bridge and extending on the other side from the wall of the churchyard and the rector's fishpond up to the conduit of the 'Scolbrook',* i.e. the Henmore Brook.

There was contemporary concern that so many of Ashbourne's revenues were being diverted out of the town, no doubt to contribute to the enormous costs of constructing the magnificent cathedral of Lincoln. However theoretically at least Lincoln would have been obliged to pay for the upkeep or rebuilding of the chancel of the new parish church in Ashbourne, the parishioners being responsible for the nave.

By this period Ashbourne had become the head of one of six rural deaneries into which Derbyshire was divided for ecclesiastical administrative purposes. The area included most of its original Anglian parish with the addition of Hartington to the north and a line of parishes south of the Henmore and Dove stretching from Bradley to Norbury. In 1291 the annual income from the rectory was £66 13 4d (100 marks) plus £5 (7½ marks) for the vicarage, but by 1329 it had arisen to £118 (*see below*).

Construction of St Oswald's parish church

Recently listed by architectural historian Simon Jenkins as among his 40 best churches in England, St Oswald's parish church is the oldest building in the town. Constructed on a cathedral plan with a central crossing tower and aisled transepts in Early English Gothic style, building probably began in c.1220. The brown-pink sandstone was no doubt quarried in the Mayfield and Stanton area about two miles distant.

The earliest work was that of the very long chancel, which must have been substantially completed by 1241 when the church was consecrated by the Diocesan Bishop of Coventry and Lichfield, as is recorded in Lombardic script on a very rare brass consecration plate. **[Treasure no C4: Consecration plate]** It was followed by the two transepts, the crossing tower and part of the nave, built during the reigns of Kings Henry III and Edward I. These exhibit fine examples of tall paired lancet windows and slender clustered columns as well as a rare group of stained glass nativity scenes in the North Transept (mounted in a Victorian surround of 1879). **[Treasure no C3: Nativity window]** The baptismal font also dates from c.1240, situated in the nave adjacent to the site of the original south porch where substantial parts of baptism services would have been conducted. The porch was removed during the restoration of 1837-40. **[Treasure no C2: Baptismal font]**

The widening of the nave by the erection of a south aisle divided by an elegant arcade of arches can probably be dated to the 1290s. After c.1300 several large new windows in the more elaborate Decorated Gothic style were inserted, some replacing earlier lancets to admit more light. The final phase was the erection of the massive 212-feet-high tower (65m) and spire, probably as a single project. The one hundred year building campaign may well have been interrupted by events such as the baronial wars of 1266 and 1322, the recession of 1314-20, and the Black Death of 1348-9 (*see below*).

The church manor and the early development of the town

One of the most notable features of Ashbourne's town plan is that the church is not situated in the centre of the town adjacent to the market place, but at the far end of the main street, even today surrounded by fields on three sides. Examples of similar layouts from other mediaeval towns point to the fact that the church was the original nucleus and the areas around the market place were later extensions (*see below*). Details of the town plan, which still survives in essentials to this day, are shown on the map of 1547 (*see* Treasure no L3) but are best viewed on the map compiled by Mr Jones's Academy in 1830 (*see* Treasure no C14).

The Domesday evidence for Ashbourne implies there was no urban development on the royal manor apart from a small hamlet

C2
Baptismal font

1241
The nave
St Oswald's Church

The baptismal font dates from the dedication of the church (see the entry on the church **consecration** plate), and is thought to be one of the finest examples of an Early English style font in Derbyshire.

The arcading has trefoil arches with small fleur de lis between. With its three petals, this pattern was often used to represent the Christian Holy Trinity of The Father, the Son and the Holy Spirit. It is repeated in the floor tiles in the chancel.

Fonts were often raised on steps in medieval times, as it is today, but Paley's *Book of Illustrations of Baptismal Fonts* of 1844 shows Ashbourne's font standing on the floor.

C3
Nativity window

c.1240
St Oswald's Church

The lancet window in the east side of the north transept contains a set of five medieval stained glass panels dating from the time of the consecration of the new church in 1241. This may be the second oldest glass in Derbyshire and was incorporated in a new grey 'grisaille' surround by the firm of Hardman of Birmingham in 1879.

The panels show scenes from the birth of Christ. From the top:

      King.Herod orders the massacre of the innocents
      The presentation of the infant Jesus in the temple
      The three wise men present their gifts
      The three wise men meet King Herod
      The angel appears to the shepherds

After 750 years the York Glaziers Trust restored them in 1991 at a cost of £8000.

C4

Consecration plate

1241
St Oswald's Chapel
St Oswald's Church

It is unusual to have such an early record of a church's consecration, and this plate is believed to be the earliest identified English church brass. It records the dedication of the church in 1241.

Work on the present church began in the early 1200s and the chancel was complete by the time of the dedication. The nave was added in the middle of the 1200s and was extended to the south, along with a tower, in the late 1200s. The 212 (65m) feet tall spire was added in the early 1300s.

George Gilbert Scott, a Gothic revival architect well known for the Albert Memorial in London, restored the spire in 1873 and the chancel in 1876-78.

around the church. During the 1100s and 1200s this hamlet must have been developed by the Dean of Lincoln into a small 'urban' settlement supported by the revenues from the church manor. It seems reasonable to surmise that part or all of Church Street was laid out with regular sized 'burgage plots', i.e. narrow strips of land containing space for a 'toft' (house) on the street frontage with a long 'croft' or garden behind. The plots on the north reached up the slope to a back lane (Belle Vue Road) and on the south down to the brook.

There is documentary evidence to support this theory. In the Lincoln Cathedral archives is a deed of c.1220 conveying half a toft 'on the land of the church' and another document describes a dispute between the dean & the prominent de Mapleton family as to whether their tofts belonged to the church or not. Some years later in c.1270 Henry de Mapilton & Lettice his wife granted to Richard Cook *'part of a toft in Esseburne which Roger son of Joce held upon the land of Esseburn church between the land of Robert at the Cross and the land of Nicholas de Mercinton'*.

Evidence from the Royal Enquiry of 1275
In 1274-75 the newly crowned King Edward I ordered a major enquiry into the customs and income of the crown estates, challenging tenants to demonstrate *quo warranto* (by what warrant) they held their rights and privileges. These were based on the testimony of local jurors for each hundred or wapentake and recorded on the Hundred Rolls. The Derbyshire sessions were held in Derby, where ten sworn jurors from the 'royal borough' of Ashbourne were required to deliver 'The Verdict of Esseburn'. These records contain considerable detail about the mediaeval development of the town.

Although the Latin descriptions are not always clear in their meaning, their verdict appears to say that anciently the king was lord of the whole area and received the rents of all the property, but during the reign of an unknown king, Ashbourne church *'was endowed with the rents of half the tofts'* which were then existing. This must refer to the grant to Lincoln by King William II of the church of Ashbourne with attendant property in 1093; the jurors would have been unsure of the exact date as it was in 'time immemorial', i.e. beyond their memory.

The location of these tofts is described as *'from the house which was William Spendlove's up to the land of Henry of the Cross on one side'* and *'from Balloc[th]orn up to the said cattle shed (bovariam) of the lord king'* (translations of original Latin). The first description may represent part of Church Street, as both it and the Mapleton family grant (above) refer to a cross; this may well be the one at the Dig Street junction depicted on the 1547 map (*see Treasure no L3*).

The church manor estate in 1329

A valuation of the dean's Derbyshire estates in 1329 contains much detail about the full extent of his Ashbourne lands and their value. It shows that here he owned a house, two gardens and crofts, all probably for his bailiffs and workers, as well as rents totalling nearly £6 from tenants of land and houses in Ashbourne and Hognaston.

His main land holdings on his demesne (i.e. farmed directly by his servants) were two 'carucates' of arable presumably scattered in strips at Underwood, Mapleton and 'Methley' (a lost location between Ashbourne and Hanging Bridge), twenty-two acres and one rood of meadow in Ashbourne and half an acre at Mapleton, all of which produced nearly £10. There was also an enclosed pasture at Ashbourne and the 'Lampemedewe' at Sturston - a meadow whose rent funded a church altar lamp.

Other farms were some distance from the town at Hognaston and Parwich. There were also sheepfolds at Parwich and Mapleton yielding some £32 from the sale of wool and lambs. Other income came from his water mill at Ashbourne and no less than £58 from the tithes of corn and hay (i.e. one-tenth of each farmer's annual crop) from the whole estate. His total income amounted to £118 – compared with approximately £125 from his estates at Chesterfield and £79 from Wirksworth.

The Ferrers family and the baronial manor

That part of Ashbourne which was not part of the church manor formed the Ashbourne Manor, originally owned by the crown until King John granted it to the baronial family of (de) Ferrers in 1203. It became what historians call a 'seigniorial manor', i.e. belonging to a baron or other lord, and will be referred to hereafter as the baronial manor.

After the Conquest much of the area south of Ashbourne had come into the hands of Henry de Ferrers, a Norman knight with estates throughout England. His principal seat was the castle he built at Tutbury some twelve miles away on the Staffordshire bank of the lower Dove valley. The two were linked by the postulated British and Roman trackway mentioned earlier, described in a deed of 1287 as the '*kings highway leading from the town of Esseburn' towards Tuttbur'*.

Ferrers was also granted nearly every Derbyshire village in the lowland countryside between Tutbury and Ashbourne, together with some five upland villages east of Dovedale as far north as Hartington. This included Sturston (with 'Fenton'), on the opposite side of the Henmore from Ashbourne east of Compton, although not Clifton west of Compton, which had been granted to another baron, Ralph Fitz Hubert.

These grants had dramatically changed the political landscape of the area. The villages found themselves under a baronial owner whose descendants became Earls of Derby. William de Ferrers II opposed John, Count of Mortain when he rebelled against his absent brother King Richard the Lionheart and helped to besiege John's castle at Nottingham in 1194. However after John's accession to the throne in 1199, he became a loyal supporter and his family's title of Earl of Derby was restored. In 1203 and King John granted William the manors of Ashbourne and Wirksworth with the whole of the wapentake, thereby bringing both the town and the outlying villages under his control.

The development of the baronial manor 1203-1266

Throughout England during the late 1100s and early 1200s numerous deliberately planned towns and villages – either totally new creations or extensions to established settlements – were promoted by landholders ranging from the king to barons and religious bodies. They were economic speculations, often accompanied by the establishment of a market, laid out with new streets lined by standard sized plots on which tradesmen could build their houses and shops. In 1276 an Ashbourne plot *in front of the market near the old cross'* was exchanged for an adjacent one 26 feet long by 18 feet wide; these may have been the local standard dimensions.

Both topographical and documentary evidence support a case for a new baronial extension to the existing Church Street development. The jurors for the 1275 Enquiry reported that *'now there are more tofts in the said township of Essebourn'... by means of improvements (approveamenta) made at the time of the King and Earl ...'*, which must refer to an extension of the existing urban area made during the time of King John and Earl William Ferrers II in the early 1200s.

The jurors went on to say that in addition several property exchanges had been made during the brief tenure of Ashbourne by Earl Robert Ferrers III between c.1260 and 1266. These presumably involved exchanging baronial plots with the Dean of Lincoln's church plots along Church Street, thus enabling the creation of an expanded single borough.

The new borough boundaries enclosed an area of only some 55 acres, as shown on both the 1830 map (*see* Treasure no C14) and the Ashbourne Tithe Commutation Map of 1846; they agree with a written Duchy of Lancaster perambulation of 1637 and must represent the original medieval plan. This purely urban area was obviously intended primarily for merchants and craftsmen and its former farmland was now regarded as being in Offcote & Underwood 'township' (civil parish).

The extended town plan and new market place

The extended town plan resulted in the creation of a new street – St John Street – as an eastwards continuation of Church Street and so named as it led to a *'sick hospital at the head of the town'* dedicated to St John the Baptist.

Part of this street formed the lower side of a very large new triangular market place, surrounded by numerous burgage plots stretching south to the brook, north to a back lane (now Union Street), and east to another back lane (now Hall Lane).

This space has subsequently been reduced in size by infilling with random buildings (*see below*) and thereby divided into three areas – the present Market Place, Victoria Square ('The Butchery') and the south east corner with St John Street   In order to gain an impression of the mediaeval market place, one must imagine it with all the island blocks of buildings swept away and a large open space suitable for livestock sales stretching down the hill from Buxton Road to the modern Green Man complex.

A number of other minor lanes such as Mutton (*i.e. Sheep*) Lane (now King Street) – first recorded in 1229 – connected this basic nucleus with the common pastures to the east.

The possible origins of Dig Street

Among various transgressions reported by the juror at the 1275 Enquiry was the claim that both John, the former vicar of Ashbourne, and Peter de Wynton, the current vicar, had obstructed *'the high way at Loneditch'* (or *'Loveditch'*) *'where four men of Mapleton used to carry …. dead men to the church at Essebourn'*, a rare and early mention of a 'coffin way' or 'corpse road'. These were common in upland areas of northern England, particularly where a minister or mother church had a large parish and corpses had to be carried there from outlying villages and hamlets for burial. It was considered unlucky if the bearers deviated from the same traditional route.

The meaning of 'Loneditch' was probably 'lane ditch', implying a right of way following the line of a ditch, and the most likely location would be Dig Street which derives its name from 'ditch'. Also the obvious route from Mapleton would be via the present Mapleton Road. The 1830 map (*see* Treasure no C14) shows that these two roads are actually in alignment, raising suspicions that both roads and ditch were originally connected through the plot occupied in recent years by the NatWest Bank which leads up to Dove House Green, itself a former open green subsequently encroached on by squatter housing since the 1600s. The Church Street/St John Street/Dig Street junction would thus have been a cross roads, the location of a cross shown on the 1547 map (*see* Treasure no L3).

Such a ditch is in the most likely position to have defined the boundary between the old church manor to the west and the new baronial manor to the east. Following their amalgamation into a single borough, the ditch would have become obsolete and filled in, traffic being diverted via the Market Place. This hypothesis may however be difficult to prove.

The origins of Ashbourne market

The creation of large new market place obviously implies the existence of a market, a royal or baronial perquisite providing income from rents and tolls from stallholders and customers.

However the frequently quoted statement that Ashbourne received a market charter in 1257 is erroneous, the document in question being simply a private conveyance of a property described as *'above the market'*. The earliest definite mention is actually in 1222 when William de Ferrers complained about competition from an illegal market in Clifton manor (*see below*). In 1203 he had received the grant of a charter from King John of the manors and profits of Ashbourne and Wirksworth and the whole of the wapentake, and market rights must have been implicit within this, especially as he granted Hartington a specific market charter in the same year. Ashbourne market was therefore founded in or before 1203 either by the king or by de Ferrers.

Vital components of market trading were strictly regulated standardised weights and measures. Those of Ashbourne would be the only authorised ones in the area. For example an agreement of 1227 to share the oat tithes of Bradbourne between the priories of Tutbury and Dunstable stipulated that the corn should be measured in bushels by *'the measure of Esseburn'*.

The origins of Compton and its rival market

As mentioned above, William de Ferrers complained in 1222 that five named people were holding an unauthorised market in Clifton manor to the detriment of his market in Ashbourne. This unauthorised market was almost certainly held in Compton Street, where the roads from Derby and Tutbury met before bridging the *'Scholebook'* (Henmore Brook) into Ashbourne manor. The street formed the boundary between the manors of Sturston to the east and Clifton to the west, and their respective lords were exploiting the fact that Ashbourne, Clifton and Sturston each fell within different jurisdictions, i.e. in Wirksworth, Litchurch and Appletree Wapentakes. It seems quite probable that the abnormally wide street near the bridge indicates the site of the market.

Although the 1275 Enquiry makes no mention of an unauthorised market as such it implies that a similar situation still existed. The main culprits from Clifton were named as the Knight Hospitallers of St John, an international order of 'soldier monks' originally founded to offer hospitality to crusaders. They and their tenants – who almost certainly included the five people named in 1222 – enjoyed certain trading privileges and exemptions from bridge and other tolls. They were now accused of tempting tenants from Ashbourne to take up properties on their land and also of contravening Ashbourne's manorial monopolies of baking bread in the manorial bakehouse and of inspecting and certifying the town's measures of ale and corn.

The Hospitallers possessed a 'hospital' or 'preceptory' some four miles south at Stydd in Yeaveley township, where the ruins of their mediaeval chapel still stand. This had been endowed with property at Clifton and elsewhere by Ralph Foun in c.1190. The Old Derby Road (Old Hill) in Ashbourne was originally known as Spital Hill, no doubt a corruption of the 'ho*spital*' to which it led. In 1557 the Hospitallers still owned nine cottages in Compton, which was sometimes known as 'Little Clifton' to distinguish it from the mother village.

The jurors at the 1275 Enquiry also reported that the king was being similarly defrauded by men living on the Sturston side of Compton. In fact the name Compton is first recorded in c.1200 in a grant of a toft between two other tofts in *Campedene* in Sturston.

Other deeds of 1258 and 1275 make reference to *Campedene stret(e)*.

Compton thus came into being as a new suburb at an early date. The probable meaning of the name is the 'valley where a fight or dispute took place', which may refer to earlier disputes over this boundary territory. In fact it did not come under the administrative jurisdiction of Ashbourne until 1873; even today it is regarded as a separate entity called simply Compton.

Probable sequence of the town's development

To summarise it appears that the sequence of the town's development occurred in four phases as follows:

Phase 1. The church manor hamlet which grew out of the original Anglian religious community around the parish church. This developed both before and after the Norman Conquest into a small village with regular plots scattered either side of the modern Church Street.

Phase 2. The baronial manor's planned extension made either by King John or Earl William Ferrers in the 1190s or early 1200s. It comprised a new market place and connecting streets, all surrounded by regular plots for tradesmen.

Phase 3. The suburb of Compton in the early 1200s developed by the lords of both Sturston and Clifton on both sides of Compton Street with the intention of poaching trade from Ashbourne itself.

Phase 4. The enlarged baronial borough created in the 1260s by the rationalization of properties of the church and baronial manors' estates so as to create a single entity.

Landowners and merchants

During the 1200s the expanding new town attracted tradesmen such as millers, bakers, butchers, shoemakers, tanners, glovers, maltsters, clothmakers, and even cutlers. A few – such as Alexander the Merchant (*mercator*) and Elias the Merchant – were probably wealthy merchants trading in wool, corn or livestock with the outside world. Such men possessed the wherewithal to help finance the building of the ambitious parish church from the 1220s onwards.

A major setback to the town's development was the disastrous fire which destroyed at least part of the town in 1252. This appears in the Annals of Dunstable Priory, which had property holdings in the Bradbourne area, but provides no hint as to the reason for the destruction. **[Treasure no H2: Dunstable Annals]**

During this period a handful of acquisitive local families were building up considerable land holdings and ultimately became landed gentry. These included members of the Cokayne, de Mapleton, de Bradbourne, de Marchington, and de Kniveton families, who all feature frequently in property dealings both within the town and in the Offcote and Bradley areas. The Knivetons, who settled at Bradley with a later branch in Mercaston, were particularly aggressive in their pursuit of property and wealth.

However it was the Cokaynes who were eventually to become pre-eminent in the town. Their origins are not clear, and despite claims by Victorian genealogists that they were resident in the town as early as 1150, they do not appear in surviving property transactions or other documents until after the 1250s. The beginning of their rise may have begun with a marriage into the family of Alexander the Merchant, followed by their appointment as chief bailiffs of the town and later – in the 1320s – as lessees of the manorial rights under the Earls of Lancaster, making them the effective lords of the manor.

The rebellion of Earl Robert de Ferrers, 1264-66

The Ferrers ownership of Ashbourne lasted for only some fifty years. Earl Robert de Ferrers III (c. 1239-1279) did not come of age until 1260 but shortly afterwards joined Simon de Montfort's baronial rebellion against King Henry III. As a consequence Prince Edward (the future King Edward I) led his troops into Derbyshire and Staffordshire in 1264, pillaging the Ferrers estates and destroying Tutbury castle. He demanded £200 to spare the wapentake of Wirksworth and Ashbourne; the Dunstable Annals record that the prior of Dunstable also had to contribute £10 towards this, as no doubt did all property owners in Ashbourne and district.

Ferrers retaliated and launched attacks against neighbouring supporters of the crown. Roger Cokayne complained of his depredations on his lands in Clifton, Kniveton, Ashbourne, Compton, and Underwood *'on occasion of the disturbances'*. The town did not escape, as the 1275 Enquiry recorded that Ferrers had owned a granary which *'was burnt in the time of war'*.

H2
Dunstable Annals

1252
Held in the British Library

Throughout the 1200s, the Augustinian Priory of Dunstable kept a detailed journal – *The Dunstable Annals*. They are of interest to Ashbourne because the priory had extensive sheep farming and lead interests locally.

In the entry for 1252, the Annals record a '*great fire*' at Ashbourne, which '*caused much distress and many were pauperised*'.

Sadly, no other information on the 'Great Fire of Ashbourne' has been discovered.

Image: © The British Library Board
Dunstable Annals
Cotton MS, Tiberius A. x, folio 43 verso

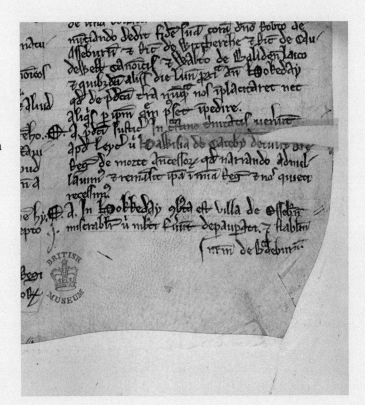

Ferrers was captured and imprisoned after the Battle of Evesham and the smaller battle at Chesterfield in 1266. His estates were ultimately confiscated by the crown and awarded to King Edward I's brother Edmund, later the Earl of Lancaster, who became one of the largest landowners in the country.

Ashbourne under the Earls of Lancaster, 1266-1322

In the aftermath of the rebellion a small group of named Ashbourne men were granted leases by the town's new owner – the king's brother Earl Edmund of Lancaster. By 1277 several burgage plots had fallen vacant and the earl leased them to nine local men for development. Again in 1286 the earl leased the markets rights for six years to another twelve named men. This could have led to this body of leading citizens being granted the status of a formal borough corporation with the right to run many of its own affairs – as happened at Chesterfield – but possibly they had failed to reverse the economic decline after the rebellion.

Earl Edmund of Lancaster had two sons – his heir, Earl Thomas, and Henry. Unfortunately Thomas became disenchanted with the rule of Edward II and raised an army drawn mainly from his own tenants and retainers to oppose the king. His account roll for 1316-17 includes payments for wages of 4d a day to sixty-two archers moved from his castle at Donington to Tutbury and Ashbourne. His subsequent rebellion resulted in his death at the Battle of Boroughbridge in Yorkshire in 1322, leading to yet another sacking of Tutbury Castle and further devastation of his lands in the area. It was however fortunate that his younger brother Henry was allowed to inherit the family title and lands, including Ashbourne and its markets.

Another Royal Enquiry of 1330 showed that Earl Henry was holding a Saturday market, which he claimed by prescriptive right as an appurtenance of the manor. Saturday markets were a particular privilege usually reserved for large towns such as Nottingham, Stafford, Newcastle-under-Lyme and Chesterfield. He also held two annual fairs – one on the Nativity of John the Baptist (24 June) and another on the feast of St Oswald (5 August), the patron saints of Ashbourne's two religious buildings – St Oswald's Church and St John's Hospital.

Family feuds and outlaw gangs

During the rebellion of 1322 most of the Lancastrian tenants and gentry had supported their lord but others remained loyal to the king, and local antagonisms lingered on. In conjunction with the weakness of royal control these resulted in an outbreak of lawlessness in the East Midlands in the early 1330s. The region was terrorised by two major gangs of outlaws – the Coterels from the Bakewell and Tideswell areas, and the Folviles from near Melton Mowbray in Leicestershire.

What is particularly notable is that the leaders were drawn from the gentry classes. The Coterel gang was led by James Coterel and his brothers, often assisted by the younger brothers John and William Bradbourne from Hulland and Lea Hall. The armed gang committed thefts, beatings and murders. They threatened the wealthy with attacks if they did not pay protection money, often writing on documents couched in the courtly language of Norman French and signed themselves as 'La companie sauvage' (i.e. the 'wild bunch').

Their most notable victim was Sir William de Kniveton who in June 1330 was killed at Bradley along with John Matkinson by James and Nicholas Coterel aided by Henry Ody of Ashbourne. In April 1331 they murdered Thomas Ithel of Stafford and William de Pare in Ashbourne, stole their armour and other goods, and then burgled the house of Geoffrey the wright and stole armour from Roger de Wandesleye at Mapleton.

The mediaeval countryside
In the countryside around Ashbourne the feudal lords such as the Fitzherberts of Norbury, Okeovers of Okeover and the Montgomerys of Cubley, all probably of Norman descent, ruled much of the surrounding countryside. Many created private hunting parks on the poorer soils such as Okeover Park, Birchwood Park near Norbury, and Hough Park at Hulland.

The Cokaynes of Ashbourne and the Bradbournes of Hulland, both of whom are represented by a series of impressive carved effigies on their tombs in the parish church, owed much of their prosperity to the holding of profitable offices under the Earldom – and later – Duchy of Lancaster as foresters or parkers of the forest known as Duffield Frith. This large tract of waste land, whose western pale lay a few miles to the east of Ashbourne, was used for the rearing of herds of cattle, sheep, deer and horses. Within this area there were virtually no ancient villages, and settlements such as Turnditch and Hulland Ward did not come into being until Tudor times, the latter taking its name from one of the six administrative 'wards' into which the Frith was divided. Here also early industrial development took place. Primitive iron and steel making was carried on near Hulland in the 1300s and possibly provided raw materials for the manufacture of cutlery in Ashbourne.

Further north in the limestone country, the mining, smelting and selling of valuable lead ore may well have involved some of the town's merchants; an important royal enquiry into the customs of the Peak lead mines was held at Ashbourne in 1288, almost certainly in the parish church.

Throughout the Peak District both lay and ecclesiastical landowners established vast ranches for sheep, whose wool was exported by merchants to clothiers in Flanders and Italy. The largest sheep farm was that of the Duchy of Lancaster in the Hartington area, which kept nearly 5500 sheep in the early 1300s, but the rest – known as 'granges' – were principally owned by monasteries. Musden Grange at Ilam belonged to Croxden Abbey near Uttoxeter and Hanson Grange near Alsop to Burton–on–Trent Abbey. Other owners were based further afield. Newton Grange near Tissington belonged to Combermere Abbey in Cheshire and Dunstable Priory in Bedfordshire controlled extensive sheep walks around Bradbourne, Ballidon and Aldwark. The Dunstable Annals record that 800 sheep died in Ballidon in 1243 but by 1284 there was a flock of 1200. As mentioned above the Dean of Lincoln Cathedral enjoyed the profits of his sheepfolds at Mapleton and Parwich which were part of Ashbourne's church manor.

During the 1200s England had mainly enjoyed a favourable climate and sustained economic growth, but this came to an abrupt end in 1315-22 when harvest failures and outbreaks of disease among both sheep and cattle caused near famine conditions and an economic recession. Manorial income from the Lancaster's Tutbury estates fell by 30% between 1313 and 1321 and some land was left uncultivated. This however paled into insignificance with the onset of the disastrous European-wide plague known as the Black Death in 1348-49 when between one-third and one-half of the population died. The resulting shortage of labour resulted in much Derbyshire arable land being enclosed for livestock rearing and landowners leasing farms to tenants rather than farming them directly in demesne.

The later Middle Ages
Towards the end of the 1300s the Lancastrian lands based on Tutbury Castle passed by marriage to the nobleman John of Gaunt who became Duke of Lancaster, and Ashbourne profited from his interest in the area. A new large east window in 'Perpendicular' style was inserted in the chancel of Ashbourne church and filled with heraldic stained glass in the 1390s to commemorate local Lancastrian families. The central shields depict the coat of arms of Henry, Duke of Lancaster, who died in 1361, and his son-in-law John of Gaunt, who died in 1399. Other shields include those of Audley, Blount, Pole and Okeover who served in John of Gaunt's knightly retinue. **[Treasure no C5: Heraldic shields]**

However on Gaunt's death in 1399 King Richard II disinherited the son and heir Henry Bolingbroke, the new Duke of Lancaster, who raised an army and forced the king's abdication. He was thus able to regain his lands and to ascend the throne as King Henry IV. Subsequently the Duchy was absorbed into the Crown estates but retained its separate identity and administration. Thereafter the Tutbury and Ashbourne properties became royal possessions.

The foundation of chantries in the parish church

Some wealthy mediaeval landowners, worried about the salvation of their souls in the afterlife, founded chantry chapels in their parish churches. These were areas with a separate altar where a priest could be employed to chant prayers forever for the souls of specified members of their family to hasten their journey to heaven.

In the 1390s two members of the Kniveton family of Bradley founded chantries in Ashbourne church. About a hundred years later in the 1480s John Bradbourne and Ann his wife founded another chantry, probably in the South Transept. Following John's death his widow remarried John Kniveton, and made new provisions for its endowment and for the safe keeping of its records. **[Treasure no H3: Will of Ann Kniveton]** Many such chantries would have had painted wooden altars often taking the form of a 'triptych' with a central panel and folding side wings, all painted with religious scenes. One such example – although not original to Ashbourne church – is that depicting St Michael and the 'Man of Sorrows' dating from the same period. **[Treasure no C6: St Michael and the Man of Sorrows]**

C5
Heraldic shields

c.1392-1399
St Oswald's Church

These three rows of nineteen heraldic shields are visible at the top of the east window above the main altar. They are survivors of a much larger series dated between 1392-1399 and were incorporated in a new window design by famous stained glass artist Charles Kempe in 1896.

The top two shields are the arms of Henry, Duke of Lancaster, who died in 1361, and his son-in-law John of Gaunt, who died in 1399. The House of Lancaster held Ashbourne from about 1266. Other shields include those of Audley, Blount, Pole and Okeover who served in John of Gaunt's knightly retinue. The window was commissioned by Major Andrew George Corbet of the Grove Hall near Offcote as a memorial to his wife Mary, née Adderley. The Corbet & Adderley arms are the bottom left hand shield.

H3
Will of Ann Kniveton
c.1500

Ann Kniveton, who died around 1500, established a chantry chapel in the parish church. This was an area with a separate altar where a priest could be employed to chant prayers forever for the souls of her first husband John Bradbourne and herself. The costs were covered by income from investments in property. This extract from her will shows her instructions for making a chest with three locks to house all the deeds for both this chantry and another she had founded in 1480 at her home at Hough Park near Hulland.

After Henry VIII abolished chantries in 1547, the chest probably stayed in the church until Queen Elizabeth's Grammar School was founded in 1585. It was then used for the storing the school charter and other documents and remained in the keeping of the school until sold in 2000.

C6
St Michael and the Man of Sorrows

c.1500
Painted panel

This panel probably formed the left wing of a folding 'triptych' or altarpiece, and was designed to illustrate the power of 'indulgences'. These were licences or dispensations issued by mediaeval priests intended to speed a person's soul to heaven.

Christ is shown as the 'Man of Sorrows' or the 'Image of Pity' above a Latin indulgence inscription. His half-length figure is set against a brocade background. St Michael, below, wearing a red cope like a cloak, impales a dragon with his cross-staff. On the reverse is a grey full length female figure, her left hand raised and a blank speech scroll above. The painting shows Flemish influence.

The panel was the gift of the Rev Thomas James Jones, rector of Atlow near Ashbourne, to the vicar of Ashbourne about 1874. He is believed to have been rescued it from Tideswell Church where he had been curate in the 1860s. It was exhibited at a major exhibition of medieval art at London's Victoria & Albert Museum in 2003.

Tudor & Stuart period (c.1540 – 1660)

Ashbourne town in 1547

By the early 1500s Ashbourne was well established as one of the major market towns of Derbyshire, yet it was still very rural in nature, and probably supported little more than 500 people, or a hundred families.

The extremely fortunate survival of a pictorial map of c.1547 provides a valuable illustration of the physical appearance of the town as it had been in the late mediaeval period. **[Treasure no L3: 1547 map]** Most of the houses are low one- or two-storey timber-framed buildings, one of which still survives as the fish and chip shop in the Market Place, dated by tree-ring samples to 1420.

Only on part of the east side of the Market Place are illustrated any larger buildings. Here they were of two or even three storeys, with high gable-ends facing the market. The buildings on the north side of Church Street, continuing up one side of Victoria Square to the top of the Market Place, appear to form a regular pattern of alternate fronts and gable-ends facing the street or market, but this is probably an oversimplification by the survey or of the actual situation.

Today, only the occasional gable-end remains fronting the market, such as that of the restaurant at the end of Tiger Yard in Victoria Square. This is timber-framed building with a projecting upper storey which has been also dated by tree-ring samples to 1493. The extension of this building backwards in Tiger Yard reveals exposed timbers. The Gingerbread Shop in St John Street has similarly been dated to 1492.

One of the most interesting features of the map is that it illustrates the early stages of the infilling of the Market Place with buildings, a process that has taken place gradually over the centuries. The haphazard development of buildings that now divides the old Market Place into separate areas forms a direct contrast to the regular planning of the original town, and consists of a series of irregularly aligned buildings intersected by narrow alleys bearing such picturesque names as the Middle Cale and The Gallery. Anciently, all this block was known as The Middle Cale – the middle plot of land – and many of the buildings here are the direct descendants of the mediaeval market stalls. As in Tudor London *'stall boards were of old time set up by the butchers to show and sell their flesh meat upon, over which stall boards they first built sheds to keep off the weather, they grew to shops and little by little to tall houses.'*

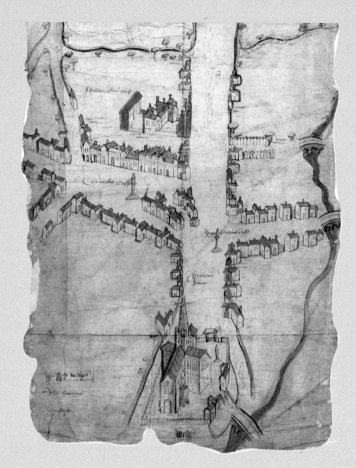

L3
1547 map

Map of Ashbourne
Surveyor not known
The National Archives

The earliest known plan of a Derbyshire town, this map is a bird's eye view from St Oswald's Church. It was drawn for use in a dispute over land enclosures.

This section of the map shows a small town built around a triangular market place with regular houses placed along the streets with burgage plots (medieval crofts) behind. This medieval town plan is still evident on the ground today.

Many houses follow an alternating front-on and side-on pattern, still seen in the Gingerbread Shop in St John Street and the Lamplight Restaurant in Victoria Square, which were erected before this map was drawn.

The Ashbourne map illustrates this process at a halfway stage; two blocks of property – stalls with chambers over them – are shown divided by a space that could be the present Gallery. As all this infilling is today on the south side of the old Market Place, this must have been the original site of the market stalls which are frequently mentioned in mediaeval records. By 1314 the town had twenty-two of a permanent nature although by the 1400s many were in decay and disrepair. The original 'Shambles' (butchers' stalls) consisted of a block of stalls surmounted by a large chamber, the whole probably supported by massive oak crucks at either end. The walls were of wattle and daub, lined internally with oak boards, and the building roofed with wooden shingles. At least by 1536 a moothall or town hall with a courthouse stood somewhere in the centre of the market place, as also did the market cross illustrated on the map.

Gentry houses

The old hall of the Cokaynes (on the same site as the present Ashbourne Hall in Cokayne Avenue) is shown on the map as a large and ambitious timber-framed structure with projecting upper storeys and a number of wings. Its entrance appears to have been by a separate turreted brick gatehouse, a fashionable addition of the late 1400s and 1500s.

On the opposite side of the road can be seen the palings erected around the park that the family had recently created. This was an addition to their other local park containing a hunting lodge (on the site of Lodge Farm) situated on the Clifton road. Both parks, along with another in Warwickshire, are commemorated by an inscription on the chest-tomb of Sir Thomas Cokayne (died 1537) in the church:

> *Three Parkes empaled eke [also] wherein to chase his deere*
> *Aloft the Lodge within this Parke he also builded here*

Sir Thomas's funerary helmet which formerly stood on his monument still survives. **[Treasure no L2: Cokayne helmet]** His grandson, another Sir Thomas, had similar interests, as he was the author of a *Short Treatise of Hunting* in 1591.

The map also shows 'Christopher Hurt's house' at the southern edge of Ashbourne Green. Part of this building with its timber

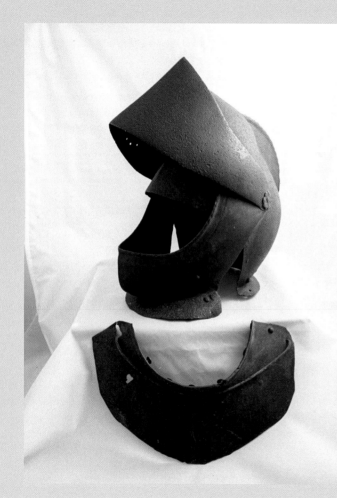

L2
Cokayne helmet

1537
Loaned by the Stainer family

This steel helmet was owned by Sir Thomas Cokayne, called "Thomas the Magnificent" by Henry VIII who knighted him at the siege of Tournay in 1513. He later accompanied his king to France in 1520 to the royal meeting on the magnificent Field of the Cloth of Gold.

The helmet is a closed-helm type from a set of field armour. This type of armour was worn in combat and was plain but practical unlike more ceremonial or jousting armour, and may have been worn by Sir Thomas in France.

After his death in 1537, St Thomas' armour hung over his grave in St Oswald's Church until the 1840s: now only the helmet survives.

frame – including an original external oriel window – is remarkably incorporated into the present Green Hall when it was rebuilt in c.1690.

This house became the home of Thomas Hurt, one of the five founding fathers of Queen Elizabeth's Grammar School in 1585. The inventory of his goods and chattels made on his death in 1610 lists a main hall and parlour, study, kitchen, buttery, larder and brewhouse, five main 'chambers' with beds, a 'serving man's chamber' and 'childrens lodgings' (with 'stuffe for childrens cot'). His study contained not only his library but also a pistol, two guns and a crossbow. He obviously lived in some style, as his 'apparrell, rapier and dagger' was valued at over £13, his bed nearly £4, and his family silver over £15. His total wealth (excluding property) amounted to nearly £160.

Tudor farming

Ashbourne Green was the town's main common pasture, remnants of which still survive as an open space. Continual disputes over the enclosure of parts of this common by the Hurt and Kniveton families to the exclusion of other users took place during the 1400s and 1500s. Livestock raising became increasingly lucrative for grazier-butchers such as Roger Jackson of Ashbourne who supplied the Vernon/Manners family of Haddon Hall with beef – some used for the minced pies for their Christmas celebrations in 1550.

Upland villages – especially those bordering the River Dove – also had extensive pastures for grazing sheep and cattle. For example in 1640 Tissington had seven separate pastures called Darfield, Hollington, Sharplow and Shaws. Stock numbers were usually limited to a specific number of either sheep walks or 'beast gaits' (the Viking word for walks) for cattle or oxen; some were shared with neighbouring settlements without intermediate boundaries. Tenant or yeoman farmers had large flocks of sheep – John Dakyn of Parwich and Thomas Charlton of Brassington each had over 250 head in the 1530s.

Most villages and hamlets continued to have open arable fields for growing crops, even in the Peak, although they were being increasingly enclosed for pasture. Evidence for this can often be seen in the ridge-and-furrow landscapes which are the fossilised remains of long S-shaped plough strips. They can be seen near Mapleton and Thorpe and especially adjacent to the A515 road at Tissington. In these limestone uplands oats were the staple crop – mainly used to make oatcakes in place of white bread, as wheat for would have been a luxury and only grown on the more fertile lowlands.

Ashbourne itself had three large common fields divided into numerous arable strips *'each of which fields used to lie fallow every third year, and to bear corn at other times'*. They were situated in Offcote and Underwood to the north-east of the town and at the time of their enclosure in c.1622 were called the Low Field, the Woodeaves Field and the 'Neighmere' or 'Naughtmare' Field (the latter now being the site of the modern grammar school). Meadowland called Long Doles was situated on the flatter river plain towards Hanging Bridge, some of which remained in strips or 'doles' down to the early 1800s.

Religious Reformation

The Reform(ation) of worship in the 1540s brought about the most dramatic change in Ashbourne's religious life. It meant the end of the ritual of Roman Catholic masses conducted in Latin, and the introduction of simpler services in English by what now came to be called the 'Church of England' under King Henry VIII, totally independent of the control of the Pope in Rome. Many colourful traditional furnishings and fittings such as paintings, window glass, statues and service books were destroyed by 'protest-ants' in protest against the rituals of the old religion. Henry VIII's Commissioners recorded copes, communion vessels and similar religious objects in Ashbourne's vestry in 1553, although they also included *'two old frocks of no value being lent to disguise persons at the bringing in of a May game'*, presumably some form of May Day mumming play.

Dissolution of the monasteries

All abbeys, priories, chantries and related religious foundations were 'dissolved' (closed) by the king and their property – including their distant granges – confiscated by the Crown. This was sold to local landowners or London-based speculators competing with each other in an unseemly scramble for monastic pickings.

Ashbourne's closest monastery – the small priory at Calwich near Mayfield – was closed and acquired by John Fleetwood from Preston; the historian Erdeswicke writing in c.1590 described it as originally *'a house of religion, now a Lancashire gentleman is owner thereof who, as I have heard, hath made a parlour of the chancel, a hall of the church, and a kitchen of the steeple'*. The adjoining monastic estate at Mayfield which had been owned for centuries by Tutbury Priory was acquired firstly by the Astons, but sold on to the Rolleston family from Lea near Matlock. The monastic farms around Bradbourne belonging to Dunstable Priory were similarly sold to Sir Anthony Babington of Dethick.

In the town itself nine houses in Compton were sold to separate purchasers following the closure of the Hospitallers' preceptory at Yeaveley in 1557. Its site at Stydd was acquired by Francis Colwich who subsequently also built a house there. A few properties in the town owned by Croxden Abbey near Alton were also disposed of.

The only ecclesiastical property to escape was the Ashbourne church manor with its tithes, now valued at over £64, which the Dean of Lincoln was allowed to keep; he leased them in 1561 to Sir Thomas Cokayne for £71 p.a. for 80 years. The parish vicar was also allowed to keep his £5 p.a. income.

Catholic recusants

Although most people went along with the change of religion it was not accepted by all. It became a major political issue as England was under constant threat of invasion by Catholic countries, and 'papists' became regarded as potential traitors to the Crown. Around Ashbourne a few prominent gentry families – known as 'recusants' (or 'refuse-ants') – remained true to the old religion, notably the Fitzherberts of Norbury & Roston, the Longfords of Longford and the Pegges and Whitehalls of Yeldersley, together with their retainers. Sir Thomas Fitzherbert spent nearly thirty years in prison for refusing to change, despite being offered his freedom if he was prepared to compromise, and died there in 1591. Their actions endowed notoriety on the whole area and in fact the petition of 1583 for founding a grammar school in the town specifically mentioned that *'for wante of scholes the youthe of that cuntrye followe the olde traditions of men and rather cleave to Papistrye than to the truthe of the gospelle'*.

The 1580s were politically a particularly tense period in Derbyshire, where the Catholic Mary Queen of Scots was kept under house arrest and where a plot to place her on the throne by Sir Anthony Babington of Dethick was discovered in 1586. In addition England was infiltrated by English Catholic missionary priests returning from special training in Rome and Douai (Belgium). They were given shelter by sympathetic gentry families who often hid them in so-called 'priest holes'. For example it was claimed by government informers that *'at one Rawlins house at Roston, before the parlour door there is a space where priests and the church stuff are to be found; there are many recusants in that place and they resort thither for mass'*.

One such priest was Ralph Sherwin, a prominent academic who had been brought up on the Longford estate in Rodsley, but was arrested soon after his arrival in England and executed at Tyburn in London in 1581; he was canonised by the Roman Catholic Church as a saint and martyr in 1970 and a modern memorial bust is displayed in Ashbourne's Catholic church. Two other priests found hiding in the Fitzherberts' second seat at Padley near Bakewell were hanged, drawn and quartered in Derby in 1588. This was the same year as King Philip II of Spain's invasion fleet known as the Spanish Armada was defeated at sea, after which the Catholic threat temporarily subsided.

Founding of the Grammar School and almshouses

Tudor Ashbourne supported a number of wealthy families, many with relatives engaged in lucrative trades in London, and it was a group of such men headed by the Lord of the Manor, Sir Thomas Cokayne, who successfully petitioned Queen Elizabeth I to found a grammar school here in 1585. A superb hand-coloured royal charter was drawn up which laid down that:

> 'from henceforth there shall be one Grammar School in Ashburne ... for the Education, Institution, and Instruction of the Boys and Youth in Grammar and other Good Learning to Continue for Ever which shall be called the Free Grammar School of Elizabeth Queen of England in the Town of Ashburne in the County of Derby'.

Subsequently a 'faire School house with convenient lodgings for a Master and Usher' was erected in Church Street in local stone, an outstanding example of Elizabethan scholastic architecture (although now converted into private apartments). Building commenced in about 1583 but was not finally completed until 1607. It comprised a central schoolroom surmounted by dormitories and attics, flanked at either end by residences for two schoolmasters. A pavement of cobbles was laid in front of the building, gathered from the bed of the River Dove near Hanging Bridge partly by the pupils themselves, who were rewarded with 18 pence worth of bread, cheese and drink. **[Treasures nos L4 & L5: School foundation charter; School matrix]**

Owing to a series of bad harvests in the last fifteen years of the 1500s, exacerbated by visitations of the plague brought increasing poverty and an increase in the number of unemployed poor, many of whom became vagabonds. The plague visited Ashbourne in 1594, 1606 and 1646. That of 1606 saw 62 deaths (36 being children) from 24 households. They included the two children of Mr Ward, headmaster of the grammar school.

L4

School foundation charter

1585
Folios and royal seal
The Old Trust/Derbyshire Record Office

The charter, granted by Elizabeth I on 17 July 1585, authorised the founding of a Free Grammar School in Ashbourne. The charter consists of three folios written in Latin and has its great seal (partly damaged) attached.

The charter has borders and initial letters decorated with painted figures and motifs, including crowns, Tudor roses, a royal coat-of-arms, a crowned eagle holding a sceptre, and clouds with rays of sun coming down.

The initial 'E' is decorated with a fine miniature portrait of the queen on her throne, with the letter E included and surrounded by allegorical figures, exotic birds, animals and fruits, attributed to Nicholas Hilliard, the foremost court miniaturist of his day.

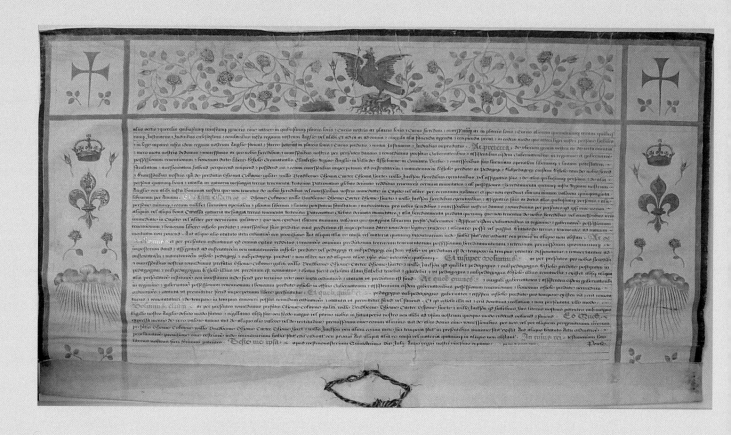

The Charges of theise lres Patentes doth amounte vnto xxviii. li.
as by the pertizulars therof hereunder written maye appeere the whiche some of
xxviii. li. Humphery Strete citizen and merchauntailour of
london borne in Asheburne in the County of Derby did geue & pay vnto the
Gouernours & assistaunte within named the xxvi daye of July in the yeare
of oure lorde god 1585.

Imprimis for drawinge the paper booke ſ———————————— xx s
Item for ingrosinge the same ſ———————————— xl s
Item to the Queenes soliciter for penninge the same ſ———— xl s
Item for gettinge the Queenes handes to the same ſ———— xx s
Item for the priuy seale ſ———————————— vi li
Item for the ingrosinge of this patente ſ———————— xlvi s
Item for the lymminge & garnishinge of the same ſ———— iii li xvi s viii d
Item for the stringe and sarsenet ſ———————— xix s iiii d
Item for the dorsett & chasewaxe ſ———————— iiii s iiii d
Item for the diuidaunte & inrolement ſ———————— vi s
Item for the patent boxe ſ———————————— vi s

Some totall is ſ———————— xxviii li xii s

L5
School matrix

c.1585
Metal alloy
British Museum

All official documents were authenticated by a wax seal. These impressions were made using a metal stamp called a matrix.

The Grammar School's seal/matrix is a 'vesica' (pointed oval) shape. The upper part shows Queen Elizabeth seated on her throne with the five petitioners for the school kneeling before her – one holds a book for learning and another a purse for money.

The picture beneath shows an Elizabethan classroom with schoolboys, masters and a group of robed governors to the rear.

The cone-shaped handle is rare. It was probably made in the Middle East or North Africa and imported through Venice.

The plight of the poor led to the foundation of several charities and almshouses, leaving the town exceptionally well endowed even to this day. The first almshouses were built in 1615-30 under the will of Roger Owfield – a London fishmonger of Ashbourne origin – and the low range of stone buildings still faces Church Street, an upper storey in similar style being added in 1848. In 1669 Christopher Pegge endowed the similar range next to Owfields at a right angle to the street.

The Owfield family – who became rich London merchants – also promoted the establishment of a 'lectureship' in 1631. This involved the appointment of a preacher independent of the vicar with the object of promoting the extreme and very strict form of Protestant religion known as Puritanism. They persuaded a group of over eighteen local gentry and London merchants to finance and maintain *one able pious, payneful, learned and orthodox preacher of the sacred word of God'* to preach two weekly sermons or lectures either in Ashbourne or in some other place within five miles in case of *'interruption'* or *'hindrance.'*

The Civil War and the Commonwealth, 1642-1660

Religious differences were one of the causes of the Civil War between King Charles I and Parliament in the 1640s, although the major factor was the stubborn and unwavering belief of the king in his 'divine right' to rule as he saw fit. This brought him into conflict with the aspirations of the gentry and merchants in the House of Commons to have a say in the government and taxation of the country

The country became divided between supporters of the Royalists ('Cavaliers') and the Parliamentarians ('Roundheads'). Derbyshire was dominated by the latter led by Colonel Sir John Gell who lived at Hopton Hall some eight miles north east of Ashbourne. Most of the local gentry who took up arms such as the Fitzherberts, Knivetons and Fleetwoods were active Royalists although Sir Aston Cokayne laid low in Tutbury Castle. Some garrisoned their mansions at different times, for example the Catholic Sir John Fitzherbert (of Norbury) at Tissington Hall and Sir Richard Fleetwood at Wootton Lodge near Ellastone.

The chief Parliamentarian protagonist from the Ashbourne area was a skinner called Captain Robert Greenwood who served as a cavalry officer under Colonel Gell and who was active in the Tutbury area; in 1662 he was described as having property at Bradley.

The town's relatively remote location largely saved it from major conflicts, although it was almost certainly raided by quartermasters – probably from both sides – collecting provisions, corn, horses and taxes for their respective armies. In this respect its position on the major London to Manchester highway rendered it vulnerable. In 1643 Sir Richard Fleetwood *did great hurt in plundering the traffique betwixt Lancashire, Cheshire and Derby, by robbing and stopping of carriers which went weekly from Manchester to London'*. A contemporary Royalist tract of 1644 celebrated Sir John Fitzherbert's capture of eighty Manchester-bound packhorses laden with match and ammunition near 'Ashbourne in the Peak'.

His actions and those of other Royalists from Bakewell were apparently keeping the country people away from Ashbourne market, and Colonel Gell despatched a cavalry squadron to the town under Major Sanders. The Royalists intended to launch a surprise attack on them whilst they were in their quarters in the town, but instead Sanders ambushed them. According to Gell's no doubt biased account Sanders *'drew all our dragoones into the lanes and hedges, and charged them: and our horse falling on the rear of them, routed them all and pursued them to the towne of Tissington, and tooke one hundred and seventy prisoners, and many of them slayne'*.

It was presumably during this skirmish that the three cannon balls now preserved in St Oswald's church were allegedly fired by Parliamentarian light artillery from Margery Bower, a hill about one-and-a-half miles away above Clifton village. Tradition maintains that they spared the church at the petition of a deputation of the townspeople. **[Treasure no C7: Cannon balls]**

Following his defeat at Naseby in October 1645 King Charles retreated through Lichfield and Ashbourne intending to regroup his forces at Newark. Again according to Gell:

'Within two dayes after oure returne, the Kinge came with three thousand horse to Tudbury, and from thence to Ashborne, where our horse fell in the reare of them, and tooke a major, much esteemed by the kinge, and twenty-five prisoners, which major was afterwards exchanged for one Major Gibb, who was major over the horse in the associated countyes, by the Earle of Manchester's letter, and soe the Kinge marched through the High Peake to Doncaster'.

C7
Cannon balls

1644
Iron
St Oswald's Church

The English Civil War of 1642 to 1653 was the most destructive in our history with a greater proportion of the population dying than in WW1.

At the beginning of 1644, Royalist troops were in Ashbourne, seizing products on their way to market. In February, they were attacked by Parliamentary forces and driven off. It is believed locally that these cannon balls were fired at the church, making holes in the west wall, but the firing stopped at the request of the townspeople.

In the autumn of 1645, Charles I's army passed through Ashbourne after its defeat at Naseby, the king staying at Ashbourne Hall.

King Charles was eventually forced to surrender and was subsequently executed in 1649. Oliver Cromwell declared the country to be a republic known as the 'Commonwealth' with himself as 'Lord Protector'. One edict passed in 1653 proclaimed that weddings should be celebrated by a civil magistrate (confusingly called a 'Parish Register') rather than in church. However unusually the Ashbourne marriages from 1655-60 were still recorded in the church registers. After the Restoration of King Charles II in 1660 much new church plate had to be found to replace that seized during the Civil War. These included two patens and a flagon given between 1683 and 1687, the latter by Sir William Boothby. **[Treasures nos C8/C9/C10: Church plate]**

Restoration period (1660 – c.1715)

Religious persecution
Following the restoration of the monarchy there was an expansion of nonconformist sects under various names such as Quakers and Anabaptists. The Quakers gained their nickname after its founder George Fox was imprisoned for blasphemy in Derby in 1647 and told the court to *'tremble in the sight of the Lord'*. At this the magistrate Gervase Bennett – a Derby merchant with an estate at Snelston – scornfully referred to them as 'quakers'. Although an essentially peaceable sect their refusal to pay tithes, church rates and other dues led them into outright confrontation with the law. During the 1660s and '70s they were particularly persecuted by the Anglican clergy, magistrates and even the ordinary people.

They kept detailed records of their 'sufferings' which included a description of an incident at Ashbourne one Sunday in 1663 when a group were gathering for a meeting in Widow Hunt's house and were set upon by *'a rude multitude … with clubs and stones'* on entering the town. Some were placed in the stocks, some in the House of Correction and others had their horses detained. Ultimately ten were excommunicated and five committed to the county gaol. It is somewhat ironic that the man responsible for ordering such persecution throughout the country – Gilbert Sheldon, Archbishop of Canterbury – had been born at Stanton near Mayfield and his family had owned property in Church Street.

One Ashbourne Quaker, John Bartram, eventually emigrated to William Penn's newly-founded Quaker colony of Pennsylvania in America in 1682-83. He was one of a group of Derbyshire men – including ones from Parwich and Brassington – who settled in the aptly-named Upper Darby County.

C8/C9/C10/C11/C15/C17/C19
Church plate

1683 to 1903
Silver and silver gilt
St Oswald's Church

St Oswald's Church has several flagons and patens, which are used for communion wine and bread. All are dated after the English Civil War (1642 to 1653). The loss of Ashbourne's church plate may relate to the passage through the town of King Charles I and his army in 1645.

On one of the patens, Christ's feet are nailed side by side rather than crossed one above the other. It may be a re-worked earlier plate.

The boxed set of 1903 was donated by the Turnbull family in memory of their daughters, who died as the result of a fire in 1901. It is believed to be by Carl Krall, a leading silversmith.

67

Houses and the Hearth Tax

The later 1600s witnessed a slow increase in population accompanied by a consequent increase in housing. All the street frontages were filled with buildings (there had been a number of gaps in 1547 – *see* Treasure no L3) and as space became scarce parts of the mediaeval crofts behind them were built up with stables, store rooms or workshops accessed by 'yards' or alleys at the side of the buildings.

The Hearth Tax assessments of 1662-1670 provide an approximate estimate of the total number of houses and of their size, as tax was calculated on the number of fireplaces (and therefore rooms). They also offer some indication of the size of the population.

The number of houses in Ashbourne itself in 1664 was about 230, but if one adds in the figures for Compton (approximately forty-five on each side of the street), the total for the whole urban area is about 320. This compares with 315 for Chesterfield. Ashbourne was the county's third ranking town after Derby and Chesterfield, slightly larger than Wirksworth and much larger than Bakewell.

Approximately 56% of the houses contained single hearths, and 34% had two or three. Only eight houses had five to eight rooms. The largest property was that of Edward Pegge, esquire (of the Yeldersley family) with ten hearths; other sources reveal that this was on the site of the later Pegge's Almshouses in Church Street. Benjamin Taylor lived in the predecessor of the Mansion a few doors away in a six-hearth house. Mr John Buxton had eight hearths and Mr Henry Kniveton had seven; Thomas Sheapy and Mrs Sleigh both had six each.

Immediately outside the town boundary in Offcote township, Ashbourne Hall – in the ownership of Sir Aston Cokayne – contained twenty-one hearths in 1670. He was the last of the Cokayne line who had lived here since mediaeval times, although Sir Aston resided mostly on his Warwickshire estates at Polesworth. He suffered financially because of his own extravagance, his passive support for the royalist cause during the Civil War, and for his adherence to Roman Catholicism. As a consequence he was forced to sell Ashbourne Hall and estate in 1671 to Sir William Boothby, who already owned the Broadlow Ash estate at Thorpe. Sir William probably rebuilt the hall, where he indulged his almost obsessive passion of book collecting, building up one of the finest gentleman's libraries in the country. The Boothby family's ownership continued until 1846.

Inns and brewing

One of the premises with the most hearths in the town was the major inn, the *Talbot,* which stood on the site of the present Town Hall and was probably acquired by the Boothbys. The angler poet Charles Cotton and his companion stopped here whilst travelling on horseback from Derby to Hartington in 1676 and ordered *'a flagon of your best ale'* from the landlord. Cotton praised Derbyshire malt and ale and also claimed that *'you may drink worse French wine in many taverns in London than they have sometimes at this house'.*

The next reference to a named inn dates from 1701 in the probate inventory of James Foljambe, landlord of the Black(a)moor's Head in St John Street, which was also owned by Sir William Boothby. The inventory shows that all the bedchambers were furnished with window curtains, chests of drawers, a looking glass, and fine linen sheets. The largest chamber with its fireplace, tables and thirteen leather chairs was no doubt the venue for meetings, dinners and other celebrations. Following the opening of the new church organ in 1710 *'at night in the great parlour at the sign of the Blackamoor's Head they made a fine concert both of instrumentall and vocal musick'.*

In common with towns such as Derby and Nottingham, malting – the process of converting barley corns into malt preparatory to its brewing into ale by local publicans – became a significant industry in Ashbourne during the late 1600s and 1700s. Several malthouses served the many public houses both in the town and in the upland area to the north.

The importance and number of local hostelries is confirmed by a War Office survey in 1686 of the quantity of guest beds and stabling facilities available throughout the country in case of military need. These show that Ashbourne had the second largest number in the county outside Derby – 135 beds and 279 stables (slightly more than Sheffield, for example). Adding in the figures for Clifton and Compton and Sturston brings the total to 142 beds and 280 stables. Although Chesterfield had a comparable 127 beds its stabling capacity was only 184.

Roads and travel

These figures no doubt reflect Ashbourne's position as a thoroughfare town on the London to Manchester route. When Hanging Bridge over the Dove at Mayfield needed urgent repair in 1617 it was described as a *'usual way of passage to all west and north* *west parts of the land'*. However the condition of the road surface often left much to be desired. In 1676 Charles Cotton's companion complained about the *'large measure of foul way'* between Derby and Ashbourne. Cotton explained this by the *'continual travel and traffic to the county town you have just come from ... and the laden (pack) horses you meet everywhere upon the way'*. The Rev. Richard Graves described Ashbourne – based on his experiences whilst a curate at Tissington in the 1740s – as `a great thoroughfare to Buxton Wells, to the High Peak, and many parts of the North'*.

Markets and fairs

It was the busy weekly markets and frequent annual fairs for horses, horned cattle and sheep which sustained the town and its surrounding area. The markets were strictly regulated to prevent fraudulent trading outside stipulated hours marked by the ringing of a market bell. The town's standard weights and measures were constantly checked and a new bushel measure for weighing corn was obtained in 1677. **[Treasure no L6: The Ashbourne Bushel]**

The area also developed a reputation for horse breeding and there were regular four-day horse fairs held in the streets. In c.1715 William Woolley commented that Ashbourne was `now an extraordinary good market town ... its fairs are many and famous for horses, etc.', and in the 1740s Richard Graves said it had *'three or four of the greatest horse fairs in that part of England every year'*. Ashbourne breeders also attended neighbouring horse fairs in Derby, Nottingham and further afield.

Farming and the cheese trade

From the late 1690s many local farms had begun to specialise in dairying, producing quality cheese for export. Cheese factors based mainly in market towns such as Uttoxeter and Ashbourne worked for London cheese mongers. Ashbourne was described in the *Universal Magazine* of 1748 as *'a small town ... and in a rich soil tho' it enjoys little or no trade, except in cheese, which is sent from here in great quantities down the Trent'* and this was repeated by other writers in 1766 and 1811. The factors bought up cheeses directly from the farms and organised their transport to warehouses on the River Trent at Wilden Ferry near Shardlow south of Derby; from here they were shipped by water to London. This was a lucrative trade and factors such as the Longden family of Ashbourne became rich landowners. Robert Longden, who lived in a fashionable house at the top of the Market Place, was described by a diarist in 1777 as *'a civil and rather spruce squire ... has an estate of this own and gets £500 a year as a cheesefactor in the country for London cheesemongers'*.

L6
The Ashbourne Bushel

1677
Brass
Loaned by Ashbourne Town Council

The Ashbourne bushel was made in brass in 1677 as the standard statutory measure of corn for farmers and traders attending the markets. It would have been chained at the Market Cross, which stood near the bottom of the Market Place. It has two handles and stands on three feet. It bears the royal arms and an inscription in relief which reads: ASHBORNE : IN : THE : COVNTY : DERBYS : 1677.

The earliest reference to the town's bushel is in 1227 when an agreement to divide the oat tithes of Bradbourne between the priories of Tutbury and Dunstable stipulated measurement by 'the measure of Esseburn'. Weights and measures were constantly checked for accuracy. This one was no doubt recast following a statute of 1670 requiring compliance with the standard Winchester Measure of eight gallons to the bushel.

Georgian period (1715- c.1830)

The Jacobite Risings of 1715 & 1745

In 1714 the English crown was inherited by a Protestant German prince from Hanover – George I – but many people supported a rival claimant – James Stuart, the Catholic son of King James II, who became known as the 'Old Pretender' to the throne. His supporters were known as Jacobites (from 'Jacobus' – the Latin form of James) and they were responsible for a failed rising in Scotland in his support in 1715.

There seems to have been considerable support for the Jacobite cause in the Ashbourne district, probably based on lingering adherence to Catholicism in villages to the south of the town. The Papist Returns of 1705-6 named twenty-five Catholic families in Norbury and some eight in the town itself. Ashbourne and Uttoxeter were two market towns where pro-Jacobite riots broke out in 1715, with attacks aimed at nonconformist groups. A regiment of the Prince of Wales' dragoons was quartered in the town in June 1716, who may have been sent restore order.

In 1745 James' exiled son Charles Edward Stuart – known as the 'Young Pretender' or 'Bonnie Prince Charlie' – invaded Britain from France with the intention of taking back the throne by force. When news of his landing in the Scottish Isles reached Derbyshire panic set in and the Duke of Devonshire raised a volunteer regiment (the Derbyshire Blues) financed by public subscription. Substantial contributions were made by five esquires, five gentlemen, two clergymen, three ironmongers, a cheese factor and an apothecary from Ashbourne and district. In the event the regiment marched away into Nottinghamshire and made no attempt to confront the enemy!

The Prince's army, made up mainly of Scottish Highland gentry and their retainers, crossed into England and marched south via Manchester, Leek and Ashbourne, plundering supplies from shops and livestock from local farms. An eye-witness account recorded that :

On Tuesday, the 3rd of December, 1745, at night, the vanguard of the rebels came from Leek to Ashbourn. They were in number about 2000 horse and foot. On Wednesday morning they proclaimed their Prince at the Market Cross, and then proceeded to Derby. On the same day another body came - almost 8000 horse and foot. Their Prince, who was on foot, baited [i.e. took refreshment] at the Three

Horse Shoes in Compton …. There were many fine men amongst them, especially in the vanguard, which had a very fine appearance. The main body of Highlanders marched six or eight abreast accompanied by bagpipers, followed by some fifty covered wagons and over a dozen heavy cannon. According to tradition many people lined the Derby road out of the town wearing white Jacobite cockades and cheered the army as it passed.

At Derby the Prince was forced into the reluctant decision to turn back, as their expected support from the English gentry had not materialised:

On the following Friday the whole body returned to Ashborne (which placed the inhabitants in the utmost confusion). They stayed all night, and on Saturday morning, to our great joy, they marched towards Leek. The Prince and his retinue quartered at Ashbourn Hall on their return from Derby ... As the rebels went through they behaved better than expected, but as they came back they were very insolent and impudent.

During their stay in Ashbourn the rebels plundered some gentlemans' houses to a great value. Two of them went to Clifton near Ashbourne and demanded a horse of one Humphry Bown; upon his refusal they shot him dead on the spot, and then took to their heels. (Bown was an innkeeper at Hanging Bridge in Clifton civil 'township').

Apparently the rebels threatened to torch the town and were only prevented by the intervention of the Prince himself. Had they done so the outcome could have been disastrous as many houses still had thatched roofs. On the Friday night the rebels mounted guards both in the Market Place and *'at the end of the street that leads to Derby'*. To protect their rear from attack the turnpike tollgate at the top of Spital Hill was guarded overnight, and two mounted patrols were sent out to watch both the Derby and Tutbury roads. Another group spent the night at Upper Mayfield.

The disillusioned Jacobite army retreated to Leek and on into Scotland, where they were totally annihilated at the Battle of Culloden early in 1746, Prince Charlie escaping back to France.

The legacy of the invasion in Ashbourne was continued unrest. Within the next two years there are references to government troops quartered in the town presumably to keep the peace. In 1747-48 at least five dragoons from Lord Mark Kerr's Regiment or soldiers in Colonel Fleming's Regiment are recorded in the parish registers as marrying local girls. Richard Graves described a probably true heated political argument between a Jacobite barber and a nonconformist baker. The context for this was that *'the town of Ashbourn, since the late march of the rebels through that place, being divided into two parties (who persecuted each other with great violence)'*.

Problems at the Grammar School

Owing partly to the insufficiency of the original endowments, the Grammar School suffered many vicissitudes during the 1700s, with the numbers of pupils rarely rising above forty, and frequently falling short of that. One headmaster, the Rev. William Langley, was particularly troublesome to the Governors as he refused to teach the free scholars, took numerous private pupils, and made life intolerable for the second master. In 1754 one of them complained of the head's *'various and frequent interruptions of his privileges as Under Master and particularly that of Tuesday last in breaking a table placed in the school for the improvement of scholars in writing and accounts . . . and of forcibly throwing it into the school passage'*. It was around this time that the Governors appear to have mislaid their original seal matrix and had another made. **[Treasure no L7: School matrix]**

The great Georgian rebuilding

Soon after the Restoration of 1660 a wholesale rebuilding of the town commenced, and brick gradually came to replace timber-framing and lath-and-plaster as Ashbourne's chief building material. Although development was random, in a little over a century it effected a complete transformation in the town's appearance. Already by c.1715 William Woolley could write: *'it is now an extraordinary good market town and much improved in buildings, which makes it well inhabited by gentry as well as good trades'*.

Probably the earliest of the new brick buildings in the town itself was The Mansion opposite the Grammar School in Church Street, built in the 1680s (although its street frontage was completely altered in the late 18th century) by Benjamin Taylor, a wealthy attorney. There was much re-facing of older structures at the same time, and to this day a great deal of timber-framing remains concealed behind nondescript brickwork. As mentioned above, Ashbourne Green Hall was rebuilt in William and Mary style in c.1680-90 but encasing a Tudor timber-framed house inside it.

Within the town, Nicholas Spalden's Almshouses of 1723-4 were built round three sides of a courtyard next to the parish church. Although still following older Tudor traditions in their mullioned windows they incorporated the newer fashions of brick walls and

L7
School matrix

Possibly mid-1700s
Silver
Old Ashburnian Society

It is not known when or why this copy of the school matrix was made, but it is believed to be Georgian. It repeats the design of the original but with a different handle. In place of the original's cone-shaped handle, this matrix has two lions rampant supporting a crown held between the front paws.

It repeats the possible Latin spelling error of 'Gramaticalie' instead of the more usually accepted 'Gramaticalis'. A third matrix, which is still in use by the Ashbourne Old Trust, has the 'correct' spelling.

The Old Ashburnian Society purchased this matrix in 1988 following a public appeal.

hipped roofs. Shortly afterwards followed a series of extremely large town houses, mostly in Church Street, many with adjacent coach houses, the predecessors of modern garages.

The first of the Georgian-style buildings must have been two adjacent houses in Church Street – no. 28, of seven uniform bays, and nos. 24 and 26 built as one. Of mid-century date is the fine frontage of the Green Man Hotel in St John Street, built as an inn with a coach entrance to the covered court, and a 'gallows' sign reaching across the street. The second half of the 18th century saw the new fashion firmly established, and more rebuilding followed in this very urbane style, transforming much of Church Street and St John Street into period pieces of Georgian architecture. Notable examples of this period are Vine House (no. 15), the stone-faced Grey House (no. 61) and the Ivies (no. 49) all in Church Street, and St John's House (no. 54) in St. John Street. Both the erection of The Grey House and the contemporary re-fronting and altering of The Mansion opposite in the 1760s were probably the work of the Derby builder-architect James Pickford; the octagonal drawing room of 1763-4 in The Mansion is of exceptional splendour for a house of its size.

The Mansion was the home of Dr John Taylor, an old school friend of literary celebrity Dr Samuel Johnson who frequently stayed here with his biographer James Boswell. Boswell described Taylor as a *'wealthy well-benificed clergyman'* whose *'size and figure and countenance and manner were that of a hearty English squire, with the parson superinduced,'* observing that *'his talk is of bullocks'.* In 1774 Johnson's friend Mrs Thrale neatly summarised his character and lifestyle in her observations about:

'…. the elegance and splendour of Dr Taylor's surroundings at Ashbourne, his fine pictures which he does not understand the beauties of, a glorious harpsichord which he sends for a young man out of the town to play upon, a waterfall murmuring at the foot of his garden, deer in his paddock, pheasants in his menagerie, the finest coach horses in the county, the largest horned cattle I believe in England, his table liberally spread, his wines all excellent in their kinds.'

Ashbourne Hall was also rebuilt in the 1780s by the intellectual lord of the manor, Sir Brooke Boothby, although in a somewhat plain and unambitious style. **[Treasure no H6: Painting of Ashbourne Hall]** The park in front of the hall was landscaped at the same time, an ornamental lake constructed, and the main Wirksworth highway running past the windows closed, forcing traffic to use the alternative route via the Market Place and Mutton Lane (King Street) to Ashbourne Green. The result can be clearly seen on the town map produced by the pupils of Mr Jones's Academy in 1830. The diverted route was not restored until the creation of Cokayne Avenue in 1922 on a slightly different line. **[Treasures nos C13/C14: 1830 map]**

H6
Painting of Ashbourne Hall

c.1806
J Farrington RA

This painting of is the earliest known illustration of the hall, which was rebuilt by Sir Brooke Boothby in the 1780s. The view shows some of the gardens and grounds that were landscaped at that time.

Joseph Farrington was born in Manchester in 1747 and died there in 1821. His particular area of expertise was pen and ink and wash drawings and he exhibited at the Royal Academy.

He kept a diary of his travels around the country and visited Ashbourne a number of times. On Tuesday 18 August 1801 he records staying overnight at the Blackamoor's Head in St John Street. His opinion of the inn was "Civil people but the house rather slovenly. Bill moderate."

C13/C14
1830 map (x 2)

Town plan
Surveyed by the pupils of Mr Jones's Academy

The pupils of Mr Jones's School at No 31 Church Street produced this detailed map of Ashbourne. The building was the Trustee Savings Bank at that time, and the bank's actuary used the first-floor room as a school.

The street layout has changed little since the medieval period (see the 1547 map). The Tudor deer park has been developed into private pleasure grounds for the hall, closing the road to Wirksworth.

As the town expanded, cottages were built behind the main houses in yards accessed by a narrow alley or a tunnel. Several yards remain in the town and can be explored.

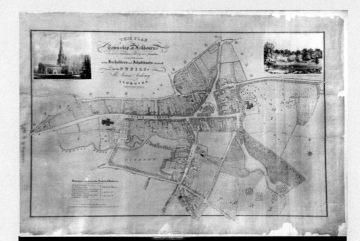

Fashionable society

In these houses lived wealthy ironmongers, tanners, maltsters, cheese factors, saddlers, lead merchants, attorneys, clergymen, and the daughters or younger sons of the neighbouring county gentry families. Through their influence Ashbourne developed as a fashionable social centre and achieved considerable repute as an adjunct to the Lichfield intellectual circle associated with Erasmus Darwin and Dr Samuel Johnson.

The social round involved numerous assemblies and dinners at the Green Man and other hostelries, card parties in private houses, and performances by travelling actors at the long since defunct theatre, enlivened by bouts of cock fighting and other amusements. The Honourable John Byng, who one night in 1789 found the inn-yard of the Black(a)moor's Head *crowded with chaises full of company, going to a grand dinner in this town'* observed cynically, *'there to be overwhelmed by dress, compliments, hams and fowls, ducks, custards and trifles, losing their time, their peace and not improving their politeness'*. Another writer similarly remarked of Ashbourne society at this period that *'card playing and squabbles about precedency occupied most of the time of the great and little gentry'*.

Despite Daniel Defoe's description of the Peak District in c.1710 as a `howling wilderness', appreciation of its 'awe-full' wild and rocky scenery grew throughout the century with the cult of the `picturesque'. Increasing numbers of travellers came to view the spectacular limestone gorge of Dovedale or to visit the spas of Buxton and Matlock, the great private palace of Chatsworth and other `Wonders of the Peak'. Many also visited Ashbourne church, especially after 1791 to view Thomas Banks' sympathetic effigy of Sir Brooke Boothby's five-year-old daughter Penelope. The presence of literary and artistic visitors such as Wordsworth, Byron, and Constable lent a cachet to the area, similar to, though to a far lesser extent, that enjoyed by the Lake District. **[Treasure no C12: Penelope Boothby].**

Coaching days

The development of Ashbourne as a resort of polite society was assisted by the improvement of the main roads by various turnpike trusts who levied tolls for their use. The road from Derby to Buxton via Ashbourne was turnpiked under an Act of Parliament of 1738 and those to Leek and Manchester and to Wirksworth and Alfreton after Acts of 1760. Several major road improvements were made by different trusts, notably the cutting of the new Mayfield Road between Ashbourne and Hanging Bridge in 1763-64, and the construction of more gradual ascents of the Derby Road in 1783-85 and of Swinscoe Hill beyond Hanging Bridge in about 1786.

C12
Penelope Boothby

1791
Thomas Banks RA
St Oswald's Church

Penelope Boothby (1785 – 1791) was the only child of Sir Brooke and Lady Boothby of Ashbourne Hall. Her white marble tomb, sculpted in 1793, shows her asleep in a long frock. The statue is reported to have moved Queen Charlotte to tears when exhibited in the Royal Academy prior to its delivery to Ashbourne.

Penelope was said to have knowledge of four languages – English, French, Italian and Latin – and the tomb has inscriptions in all four. The death of his daughter led Boothby to leave both his wife and Ashbourne Hall. He spent the remainder of his life on the Continent, dying in poverty in France in 1824.

The 1738 Act provided an alternative route to Manchester via Buxton rather than Leek and in 1789 James Pilkington could write that *'Ashbourn, being situated on the great road which leads from Derby to Buxton, Macclesfield and Manchester, derives considerable advantage from the company who travel this way'*.

This was also the impetus for the improvement of travellers' accommodation. The Green Man, a large new purpose-built coaching inn in St John Street, was erected in c.1750 probably by John Hayne, esquire, of Ashbourne Green Hall. The ancient Talbot Inn in the Market Place tried to compete and in 1752 advertised the facts that it had stabling for an astonishing hundred horses as well as a post chaise for hire. It was almost certainly owned by Sir Brooke Boothby of Ashbourne Hall who appears to have closed it in c.1785 while he was refurbishing his other property – the Black(a)moors Head – a few doors away from the Green Man.

In 1806 four post coaches ran to and from London inns daily. The *Defiance*, the *Cornwall* and the *Royal Mail* all called at the Green Man, the *Dart* at the Black(a)moors Head, and the *Telegraph* at the White Hart in Church Street. The roads were also used by the great broad-wheeled covered wagons of goods carriers such as Bass or Pickford which lumbered through the town to and from the expanding Lancashire textile region. In 1806 Pickford's wagons ran via Leek to and from London and Manchester daily, calling at the White Lion in the Market Place.

Coach travellers were occasionally subject to robberies. One of the most notorious instances occurred one Thursday morning in July 1780 when the Manchester coach from Buxton to Ashbourne was held up by a young highwayman near Newhaven who robbed the passengers of about £7. He was chased to Ashbourne by two haymakers who had witnessed the crime and caught in a public house at Low Top (Buxton Road), probably the Bowling Green. He was subsequently sentenced to death for this and other crimes.

In a very late attempt to improve coach services from Birmingham to Sheffield a new turnpike road was built between Ashbourne and Bakewell following an Act of 1811. This was a remarkable feat of engineering as, with the exception of two short stretches, its route cut an entirely new line through the countryside. From Fenny Bentley it followed the course of the Bradbourne Brook before climbing up to the summit of Longcliffe Hill in a series of bends designed to level out the gradients; other similar new sections were built between Winster and Haddon Hall.

French prisoners of war, 1806-14

During the Napoleonic Wars with France from 1802 to 1815 large numbers of prisoners were billeted on parole in different parts of the country, and Ashbourne was one of the chosen inland towns along with Lichfield, Leek, Chesterfield and Ashby-de-la-Zouch.

The prisoners were initially chiefly naval personnel drawn from all ranks. Aristocratic officers were allowed to bring their servants and, occasionally, wives, and were regularly supplied with money by their families in France. The prisoners were mainly French but some were from Prussia, Norway, Poland and Italy, and very few spoke English. The numbers held at any one time were usually about forty to fifty, but by 1810 this had increased considerably with an influx of army officers captured in Spain or the Netherlands.

As parole prisoners they were not held in a prison but lodged with local people, either in private residences or public houses. During the day they had the freedom of the town but were subject to a curfew every night, being required to be in their lodgings by 5pm in winter, 7pm in spring and autumn, and 8pm in the summer, and to remain there until 6am the next morning. These times were signalled by a church bell rung by the parish clerk. Posters were displayed to inform the local inhabitants that all prisoners *'are permitted to walk on the great turnpike road within one mile of the extremities of the town, but they must not go into the fields or crossroads'.*

The first group of forty-four officers and one servant arrived by covered wagons from Devon in December 1803. Fourteen more arrived in February 1804, among them General Rochambeau, two fellow generals and their entourage of six servants. They had been captured after the failure of a French attempt to recover one of its West Indian colonies – the island of Santo Domingo (now Dominican Republic).

Other prisoners arrived at irregular intervals, the final total being 172 between 1803 and 1814. Because they were not strictly policed several attempted to escape – twelve successfully and ten unsuccessfully between 1809 and 1812. For example N Saillard, the mate of a captured privateer called *L'aimable Nellie,* absconded in 1810, probably in a Pickford's wagon bound for London.

Inevitably there was considerable fraternising between the prisoners and the female population of the town, especially when they shared lodgings. In 1805 one of the most senior officers, General Pageot, began an affair with one of the daughters of the military Bainbrigge family of St John's House where he was lodging; he was hastily transferred to another town as he was already married.

In fact seven prisoners married local girls, including four Whitaker sisters, daughters of an innkeeper in Dig Street. One of them married 25-year-old Otto Ernst d'Heldreich, a lieutenant in a Prussian regiment fighting for the French who was captured after a major British land-and-sea victory at Flushing in Holland in 1809. Despite his aristocratic upbringing in Saxony he chose to remain in Ashbourne at the end of the war, working at menial jobs such as a painter and tobacco cutter before moving to Derby in c.1840 to work as a varnish maker. He died there in 1849, leaving numerous descendants in the area today.

Another prisoner who remained was Olav Petersen, a Norwegian press-ganged onto a French ship which was captured by the British. Anglicising his name to John Peterson he found work with the Dawson family of maltsters and became a devoted attender at the parish church, eventually becoming its verger. A flat slate memorial extolling his life and piety erected after his death in 1846 can be seen outside the south side of the chancel.

By 1815 all the prisoners who wished to leave had been repatriated. Confusingly at the same time the county magistrates in Derby decide to build an overflow House of Correction in Ashbourne. A new prison block with barred windows with an adjacent governor's house was built at the foot of New Derby Road opposite the Sion Independent Chapel. John Langford, the former overseer for the French prisoners was appointed as its governor. It only remained in use for about fifteen years and the house (later called Walton Bank) was sold into private hands. Unfortunately this train of events gave rise to an erroneous story that the prison housed French prisoners who were employed in constructing the new Derby turnpike road. Although this contains several grains of truth, in fact the turnpike was completed in 1785 long before the French arrived, and the prison was built soon after they had left!

The Industrial Revolution

The end of the 1700s witnessed not only a rapidly rising population but also the onset of what has been termed the 'Industrial Revolution', partially led by inventors and entrepreneurs from Derbyshire. In 1771 Richard Arkwright opened his pioneering water-powered cotton-spinning mill some twelve miles away at Cromford in the Derwent Valley. Soon after two similar mills were constructed on the Dove near Hanging Bridge and another three miles north of Ashbourne on the Bradbourne Brook at Woodeaves, all in entirely rural settings, but few workers were drawn from the town itself.

On a lesser scale small manufacturing industries, chiefly textiles and engineering, came to supplement the usual country town trades.

To the traditional crafts of butcher, baker, wheelwright, cooper, maltster, tanner, rope maker, weaver and the rest were added those of brass and iron founder, clockmaker, wool comber, lace embroiderer, and even the occasional stocking framework knitter. Many of these operated from workshops in the yards running back from the main streets. These yards often extended up to the old back lanes and had their entrances from the street arched over, for example Smith's Yard in Church Street or Tiger Yard in the Butchery. As population expanded during the 1800s small rows of terraced cottages were also built in many yards.

Clock making

One of the most distinctive of local industries was clock making, either carried on in small workshops or in association with small brass foundries. Long case clocks bearing the names of individual makers date from the first half of the 1700s, for example that made by Shipley in 1737. **[Treasure no H4: Longcase clock]** Clockmakers were essentially family businesses which often lasted for generations. In addition to making domestic and turret clocks, there was demand for clockwork machinery for the new cotton mills by the 1780s. The trade expanded in the 1800s and developed connections with related firms in Birmingham and Manchester.

The best known of the earlier businesses was that of the Harlow family of brass founders, clock iron-work and pinion makers which was founded in the 1700s. By about 1850 the family had dispersed to larger towns and the Ashbourne works was taken over by a former employee William Davenport, in 1837 making brass cuttings and movements for thirty-hour and eight-day clocks, etc.

Another important firm was that established by the two Haycock brothers, John and Thomas. Both born in rural south-west Staffordshire, they probably learnt their trade in the nearby Black Country, but before 1826 they had settled in Ashbourne, taking over a workshop in Smith's Yard, Compton. By the 1850s they were described as clock iron (or forge) work and pinion makers, brass founders, and bellfounders. The family subsequently became noted manufacturers of clocks, turret clocks, steam gauges and general iron and brasswork in their works at The Leys off Station Street and is still involved in the business to this day. **[Treasures nos H7/H8/H9/H12/H14: various clocks]**

Population and housing expansion

There is considerable physical and documentary evidence of a building boom of working class houses in the 1780s and '90s, especially c.1780-93. In Ashbourne itself new terraces were built in the yards behind the street frontages and on the sites of former

H4
Longcase clock
c.1737
Shipley

During the 1700s Ashbourne was one of the three main centres of clockmaking in Derbyshire with more than 20 clockmaking businesses. The other two locations were Derby and Chesterfield.

The identity of Mr Shipley is still to be established. With the clock dated to the 1730s he is possibly the father or grandfather of Jonathan Shipley, (b 1753), clockmaker of Derby. Jonathan had a son and two nephews who also traded as clockmakers in Derby. Two eight day clocks produced by his nephew, James Shipley, (d.1850), had views of Ashbourne Hall painted in the arch.

This clock needs to be wound every 24 hours.

H7
Longcase clock mechanism and dial

c.1815
Robert Harlow

During the 1700s Ashbourne was one of the three main centres of clockmaking in Derbyshire with more than 20 clock and watchmakers. The other two were Derby and Chesterfield.

The Harlow family was one of these early families. Robert Harlow, great-grandson of the founder George, inherited the business in 1815. His business showed elements of mass production. The two items on display were made at two sites. He had a brass foundry works in Ashbourne, and the faces were painted in Birmingham. This type of longcase clock was made in Ashbourne and sold throughout Britain and America.

H8/H9
Mantle clock
Wall mounted clock

c.1825
Elleby family

In the 1700s Ashbourne was one of the three main centres of clockmaking in Derbyshire and continued in this vein into the 1800s.

The business started in Dig Street, Ashbourne in 1802. One family member later established a branch in Derby. Clocks have been signed with various spellings of the surname. It closed down in the 1870s.

In 1871 Sophia, widow of Henry E Elleby (d.1870) and her sister-in-law Dorothy were running the business, described as Jewellry, Watches and Clocks. By 1881 Dorothy Elleby is living in Church Street and is blind, perhaps a result of her employment.

H12
Turret clock

c.1895
Haycock and Sons

Two brothers, Thomas and John, started the Haycock family clockmaking business in the early 1800s. At one point there were two separate businesses in the town. One of them continues to operate to this day (2017).

A turret clock mechanism is one of the oldest forms of clocks. It was not designed to give the time in hours and minutes. They were often installed in church or clock towers to announce to the locality the passing of time by striking a bell on the hour.

H14
Double-faced clock

c. 1930
Double-faced clock by Haycock

Two brothers, Thomas and John, started the Haycock family clockmaking business in the early 1800s. The brothers were apprenticed to Robert Harlow and in 1826 they took over the business of Robert's cousin, Thomas Boulton Harlow.

Today Charles Haycock and his son run the business, with a grandson waiting in line.

The double-faced clocks were clearly for commercial use and not domestic use. They were used on railway platforms and large public buildings such as banks.

open greens at Dove House Green and Mutton Lane (King Street), all now demolished. Most new development took place on either side of Compton. However a row of eight terraced brick cottages dated 1797 and known as Can Alley (later Birch's Terrace in Station Street) was built at right angles to the road in the corner of an empty field. This suggests that lack of building land was less of a factor in such developments than the desire of speculative landowners to construct the maximum number of houses.

After 1801 the decennial census figures are available for both population and 'inhabited houses'. Approximate totals for the combined urban area of Ashbourne and Compton can be obtained by adding together the figures from 1801 onwards for the townships of Ashbourne, Clifton and Sturston and then deducting estimates for the rural parts of the last two. This suggests a population of about 2500 in 1801 increasing by some 27% to around 3160 by 1831, the largest rise being between 1811 and 1821 when there was 45% increase in Sturston.

This is reflected in the figures for inhabited houses, which increased from 656 in 1801 to 776 in 1831, an increase of 19%. Sturston's houses increased from 76 to 123 (30%) in 1811-1821 alone, nearly equalling Clifton which was always the larger settlement.

Nonconformist chapels

Many members of Ashbourne's working class were attracted to the simpler and less formal services offered by various nonconformist denominations. There were occasional Presbyterian meetings in the town from the 1660s and by 1715 a fortnightly meeting was being held – conducted probably by itinerant ministers – in premises in Compton. John Wesley preached publically in the town in 1755, after which a small Methodist meeting was formed. He came again in 1772, this time preaching from the steps of a house at the top of the Market Place. By this date meetings were being held in a cottage on the south side of Back Lane (Belle Vue Road). A new Wesleyan Methodist Chapel was finally built on the east side of Compton in 1822, to be superseded by the present chapel in 1880.

The Primitive Methodists, founded nearby in the Staffordshire Potteries in 1811, also gained a following in the Ashbourne area, being served by circuit preachers based at Tunstall after 1819. They were notable for encouraging itinerant female evangelists to travel around the countryside, where their preaching often attracted large crowds. The very first was Sarah Bembridge (née Kirkland) the young daughter of a Mercaston farmer, and another was Elizabeth Evans, wife of a Norbury carpenter. She became the model for

'Dinah Morris', a fictional evangelist who features in the novel *Adam Bede* written by her niece Mary Ann Evans in 1859 under the pen-name of 'George Eliot'. It was set in the Norbury and Ellastone area.

The Sion Independent Chapel was erected at the foot of the New Derby Road in 1800 along with an adjacent set of almshouses. It was founded by philanthropist John Cooper, born in poverty in Mutton Lane (King Street) and married to a servant girl from Tissington Hall, who then made a fortune as a London brandy merchant and retired to the town in 1808.

Victorian & Edwardian period (c.1830-1914)

The impact of the railways

In common with the rest of the country the 1840s witnessed a social and economic revolution largely driven by the development of railways. The coaching era ended abruptly along with many other aspects of Georgian life which were replaced by 'Victorian values'

Although Ashbourne's population grew steadily – from about 3500 people in 1850 to about 4000 in 1900 – this was a far lower rate of growth than that of Britain as a whole or of nearby expanding industrial towns, and it became virtually fossilised in its Georgian past. Only one of the two major Georgian inns – The Green Man – was still in existence, its proprietor having bought out his rival – The Black(a)moor's Head – in 1825, closed it down and added the sign to his own. The *Derbyshire Advertiser* newspaper founded in the town in 1846 caricatured the *'quiet well-to-do order of people who hate nothing so much as bustle and change'* and its proprietors along with several other ambitious tradesmen soon deserted Ashbourne for the large nearby towns.

A railway station was opened in 1852 amid rejoicings of almost religious fervour but this was only a branch line from Uttoxeter which terminated at Ashbourne. It was not until 1899 that the line was extended (through the tunnel under Belle Vue Road) across the Peak to Buxton, but was little used by through traffic. **[Treasure no C16: Painting of Ashbourne and St Oswald's Church from the south]**

Apart from the three Georgian cotton mills at nearby Hanging Bridge, Mayfield and Woodeaves only one factory of any size was built in the town itself. This was the `stayworks' or corset factory, founded as a cottage workshop in Derby Road in 1855 but replaced by

C16
Painting of Ashbourne and St Oswald's Church from the south
1852
HL Pratt

This view of St Oswald's Church in 1852 also shows the back of the old Georgian vicarage on the site of the modern church hall. On the hill to the left can be seen the new Union Workhouse with its bell tower which opened in 1848. This later became St Oswald's Hospital, which was demolished in 2015-16.

The painting was probably made to celebrate the opening of the branch railway line from Uttoxeter in 1852 and you can see the rolling stock and the goods shed, which is still standing on Clifton Road.

Henry Lark Pratt (1805-1873) was born in Derby. He was a landscape painter at Old Derby China Works but left in 1830 to work at the Minton China Works in the Potteries. Later he produced paintings of Chatsworth and other stately homes in Derbyshire, Cheshire and Staffordshire. Queen Victoria purchased a dinner service decorated with his views of Windsor Castle.

an expanded factory complex in Compton from the 1860s onwards. This drew on an existing labour force of female textile workers working mainly in their own cottages. They were mainly 'lace runners' who had hand-embroidered designs onto plain machine-made lace net supplied by firms in Nottingham some thirty miles away. In 1851 there were seventy-three lace runners in the town, two thirds of them in Compton. **[Treasure no H10: Lace shawl]**

New public governing bodies

'Reform' and 'improvement' were the watchwords of Victorian politicians, and they set about re-organising the outdated agencies of local government and public services. In common with many market towns Ashbourne had possessed no local council to provide public services other than the parish vestry meeting. This began to change when the Ashbourne Union Board of Guardians came into being in 1845 to provide for the poor and destitute of the town and district. These new Poor Law Unions uniquely crossed county boundaries and the Ashbourne Union covered sixty-one surrounding parishes in both Derbyshire and Staffordshire. Within ten years it had built a large institutional workhouse on Belle Vue Road (later St Oswald's Hospital but demolished in 2015). The board also had powers to inspect public 'nuisances' or health hazards, which were extended when it was formally designated a Sanitary Authority in 1868.

Five years later in 1873 Ashbourne was finally combined with the suburban parts of the adjacent townships of Clifton and Compton, Sturston and Offcote into a single urban area under a Local Board of Health. In 1894 this was elevated into a fully-fledged Urban District Council with wider powers of local government. Anew Ashbourne Rural District Council covered neighbouring Derbyshire parishes.

Other services were introduced by a variety of public or voluntary bodies. A gas works was built in 1840 to provide both street lamps and domestic gas lighting for the first time. A police station and lockup was built on Belle Vue Road in 1844, later superseded by another building in Station Street. A public hall was provided in St John Street in 1858, to be followed three years later by that ultimate symbol of Victorian municipal pride – a Market or Town Hall in the Market Place. In the absence of a local authority, however, it was built by a private trust made up of a small group of prominent townsmen – known as the 'Spirited Six' – whose names are inscribed on its frontage; in fact it did not pass into the hands of the council until around the 1980s.

However, despite the work of all these bodies, water still had to be obtained from a mass of private wells or a few public pumps, and

H10
Lace shawl

1851

This shawl was exhibited at the Great Exhibition in London in 1851. It was made by Catherine Cartwright who was born in Ashbourne in 1818 and appears in the 1841 census as a 'lace runner' living in Compton. She married Stanton-born wheelwright William Pegg in 1843 and they lived at 16 Derby Road, Ashbourne.

Lace running was the process of hand-embroidering the outline of a stamped pattern onto plain machine-made lace net stretched on a horizontal frame. Nottingham firms provided the patterns for female outworkers working in their own homes. In 1851 there were 73 women lace runners in the town, two thirds of them in Compton. Mrs Pegg distributed work to young women locally.

Six million people – a third of the population of Britain at the time – visited the Great Exhibition. Queen Victoria and her family visited three times. The main glass building was later moved to Sydenham in south London, an area that was renamed Crystal Palace. The shawl came back to Ashbourne and is still owned by members of Catherine's family.

as late as 1893 eight people died as a result of an outbreak of typhoid in the notoriously overcrowded Workhouse Yard on the west side of Dig Street. By 1851 such yards were occupied by rows of terraced cottages which housed nearly a quarter of the town's population. For example, ninety-one people lived in houses fronting the west side of Dig Street, but another ninety-four lived in the yards behind. Despite their physical shortcomings, however, the yards fostered a close-knit community spirit with a high degree of mutual support.

A new vicar

Forces of change were active in other spheres as well. The arrival in 1850 of a new vicar – the Rev. John Errington – shook the local inhabitants out of their complacent conservatism and forced them to confront new ideas in religious worship. He was of High Church persuasion and his attempts to end the system of private ownership of certain pews – which accompanied ownership of specific superior houses – met with considerable opposition, which became known as 'The Great Pew Battle'. He also had considerable problems in introducing cathedral-style services complete with sonorous organ, surpliced choir and colourful ritual. His attempts to dismiss the old organist and to install a new organ ended in the farcical situation in 1858 when he was forced to erect a wooden 'cage' around the organ seat to prevent its use by the old organist. New church plate was donated to the church during this and later periods. **[Treasures nos C15/C17: Church plate]**

A new lord of the manor

Many of the old gentry families of the area, including that of the Boothbys, lords of the manor living at Ashbourne Hall, disappeared in the '40s or '50s and their mansions were sold or let. A prominent landed businessman – Francis Wright – appeared on the scene and purchased the manorial rights (but not the hall). He was the immensely wealthy son of a Nottingham banker who became sole owner of the Butterley Company's vast iron and coal empire in east Derbyshire. Even though his mother was a Beresford of Ashbourne (from whom he inherited the Osmaston estate) and his wife a FitzHerbert of Tissington, he was more representative of the new industrial and commercial classes – and brought with it their ideas and values. Between 1846 and 1849 he built a new country mansion nearby called Osmaston Manor, fitted out with all the latest technology.

It was perhaps inevitable that Errington and Wright should clash over matters of religion. This eventually led to the bizarre situation when Wright – with the reluctant consent of the bishop – built a Low Church Anglican 'free church' called St John's on Buxton Road as a rival to the parish church.

Wright wielded considerable power through his chairmanship of the magistrates' bench and his ownership of the market rights. He used the former position to close many public houses, and the latter to move the weekly cattle market and the periodic fairs out of the Market Place, both on the grounds of their 'unseemly' nature, providing a new cattle market on a steep site adjacent to his new church. He became particularly unpopular with the majority of the population for his unsuccessful attempts to stop the traditional Ashbourne game of Shrovetide Football. His interference with the town's major customary festival was greatly resented, even by some members of the middle classes, and in 1861 scurrilous posters were circulated describing him as *'president of the poke-your-nose-into-everybody's-business-society'*! Nevertheless following his death in 1873, a monument was erected to his memory in the Market Place, which still remains to this day – as indeed does Shrovetide Football! **[Treasures nos H11 & H13 : Shrovetide painting; Shrovetide balls]**

Late Victorian and Edwardian growth

This episode demonstrated the strength of Ashbourne's highly independent and close-knit community spirit, which was emphasised by the founding of not one, but two local newspapers in the last years of Queen Victoria's reign, remarkable for a town of only 4000 people. The *Ashbourne News* was founded in 1891 by Joseph Osborne and the *Ashbourne Telegraph* in 1903 by Joseph Henstock. The *Telegraph* was affectionately known as 'The Stunner' – presumably an ironic comment on its absence of sensational news compared to the national press! They were amalgamated in 1957 as the *Ashbourne News Telegraph*, which still performs a vital role in uniting the community even in this modern digital age.

By the 1870s the town had begun to expand beyond its mediaeval limits, and a small number of Victorian villas were built on its fringes, mostly along the crest of the ridge on North Avenue. By the end of the century, rows of terraced houses had also appeared, particularly on the western approach roads.

H11
Shrovetide painting

1862
On loan to Ashbourne Heritage Centre

The Shrovetide Football Game was not always popular with everybody in the town. In the mid-1800s, some of the more 'respectable' inhabitants thought that the large quantities of alcohol consumed and the obstruction of the streets, brought the game into dispute. Led by Francis Wright of Osmaston Manor, attempts were made to stop the game from starting in the Market Place.

Some key supporters of the game are shown in this painting of 1862, the last year that the game started in the Market Place. Little is known of the artist except that he raffled the painting having failed to find a buyer.

H13

Shrovetide balls

Cork filled leather balls painted to a design chosen by the 'turner up'

The Royal Shrovetide Football Game is a survival of mediaeval street football, taking place annually on Shrovetide Tuesday and Ash Wednesday.

It is played between Up'ards, traditionally those from north of the River Henmore, and Down'ards from south of the river. The game is played throughout the streets, alleyways, in the river and park pond, and across fields between goals three miles apart.

The ball is usually carried around in a large group of players (the hug), but there are occasional breakaways. A player scoring a goal keeps the ball but, if no goal is scored, the ball is returned to the 'turner up'.

In 1897 Ashbourne received its long-awaited piped water supply to replace the numerous hand-pumped wells across the town. The water was obtained from a new reservoir at the top of the new Derby Road. In 1910 the Swiss-owned Nestlé Company opened a large dairy factory with its own water supply and railway sidings; milk was collected from local farms in metal churns initially by horse and cart but later by lorry. In addition the corset factory and the two Mayfield textile mills were all enlarged.

In 1899 the railway line was extended through the Peak District to Buxton, enabling milk from farms around Dovedale to be transported daily as far as London. A tunnel was excavated under the ridge behind the town and a bridge built to support Church Street, unfortunately involving the demolition of several Georgian properties. A new station (with Station Hotel) was built nearer the town centre and accessed by a new road – Station Road – constructed across The Mansion's paddock, the only substantial alteration to the mediaeval street plan.

The parish church had been extensively restored in 1837-40 by the architect Lewis Cottingham but more work was carried out by George Gilbert Scott in 1876-78. In addition in 1882 G L Abbott removed the pseudo-Perpendicular window of the nave inserted in 1840 and replaced it by a reproduction of the original mediaeval one (as seen in the engraving of c.1792) **[Treasure no H5: View of St Oswald's Church from the west]**. Several other new stained glass memorial windows were installed, the most attractive yet poignant being that designed by Christopher Whall in 1905 to commemorate the tragic death of two sisters in their early twenties. Monica and Dorothea Turnbull were the two daughters of churchwarden Peveril Turnbull and died in a fire at their home at Sandybrook Hall. **[Treasures nos C20, C18 & C19: Turnbull memorial window; Painting of Mrs Phyllis Turnbull and her daughter Monica; Turnbull set of church plate]**

H5

View of St Oswald's Church from the west

c.1792
J B Cuming

This drawing of the west end of St Oswald's Church in about 1792 is the earliest known printed view of the church. An engraving taken from it was published in the *European Magazine* in 1793.

This is an important record of the original mediaeval west window, which was replaced in 1840 by a much larger one in Perpendicular style. This was subsequently removed – probably for structural reasons – and a reproduction of the original window put back in its place.

John Brompton Cuming was born in 1772 in Fenchurch, London, and died in 1851. He exhibited at the Royal Academy a number of times. His particular area of expertise was landscapes.

C20
Turnbull Memorial Window

1905
Christopher Whall

St Oswald's Church
This window commemorates the tragic death of Monica (born 1878) and Dorothea (born 1880), the two daughters of churchwarden Peveril Turnbull in a fire at their home at Sandybrook Hall in Offcote in 1901. Dorothea's dress was set alight by an oil lamp and Monica, in trying to save her, set her own dress alight. Monica died on 4 March and Dorothea on 27 April. The father was land agent to the Sandybrook estate of Sir Horace Blakiston, and a JP.

This window is by Christopher Whall (1850-1926), a leader of the Arts and Crafts Movement. The design shows the three virgin martyrs, St Barbara, St Cecilia and St Dorothea. The faces of Barbara and Dorothea are portraits of Monica and Dorothea and it is believed that that of St Cecilia, in the centre, is a portrait of the artist's wife and the angel rising from the flames is that of his daughter.

C18
Painting of Mrs Phyllis Turnbull and her daughter Monica

c. 1882
E R Hughes

Edward Robert Hughes painted this portrait of Mrs Turnbull and her daughter Monica (born 1878). Mr Peveril Turnbull was land agent to the Sandybrook estate of Sir Horace Blakiston, and they lived at Sandybrook Hall, Offcote.

After Monica's tragic death in a fire in 1901, the parents founded St Monica's Home for Girls for the Waifs and Strays Society in Windmill Lane, Ashbourne, which opened in 1911. From about 1947 to the 1970s the home cared for physically disabled children, where the portrait hung until the home closed in 1986. It was then given to St Oswald's Church.

Edward Robert Hughes, 1851-1914, was a watercolour painter. An exhibition of his work including the Turnbull painting was staged in 2015 at Birmingham Museum and Art Gallery.

With the advent of art and science teaching in the 1890s, the old Grammar School in Church Street became increasingly cramped, and in 1907-09 a new building was erected by the County Council in appropriate 'Tudorbethan' style on a new site on The Green Road. Girl pupils were admitted for the first time – an innovative and progressive move for the period. It was formally open by the 9th Duke of Devonshire on 23rd August 1909 using a ceremonial key. [**Treasure no L8: The Devonshire Key**] George Edward Cokayne, a descendant of the principal founder of the original school – Sir Thomas Cokayne – commissioned a copy of Zuccharo's 1580 portrait of Queen Elizabeth I from the National Portrait Gallery in London, which was presented to the new school in 1911. [**Treasure no L9: Portrait of Queen Elizabeth I**]

First World War 1914-1918 and after

The outbreak of the First World War in 1914 took most British people by surprise and it was confidently assumed that it would 'all be over by Christmas'. As with other towns, military recruitment began in Ashbourne with patriotic speeches and parades and many young men joined up. However the real horrors of trench warfare in France soon became apparent as local casualties began to mount. In fact the *Ashbourne Telegraph* began a weekly feature reporting on the death or wounding of individual soldiers from all over the district, with short biographies and often photographs of each.

The town contributed to the war effort by providing convalescent facilities for wounded soldiers in the Century Hall at the Wesleyan Chapel, and also by welcoming Belgian refugees. After compulsory conscription was introduced in 1916, a panel was set up to hear appeals by local shopkeepers and farmers for exemption of their workers from service. These highlighted the difficulties of local businesses coping with greatly reduced staffing levels, but most appeals were rejected; consequently women were increasing required to take over jobs previously undertaken by men.

By the end of the war in 1918 the death toll had reached treble figures. One hundred and ten names are recorded on the town's war memorial unveiled in 1922, and there were probably another two hundred or so from local villages. Nationally the old social order was changed forever as a result of the vastly reduced labour force; servants and farm workers were often impossible to recruit and women were given more responsible permanent jobs.

L8
The Devonshire Key

1909
Queen Elizabeth's Grammar School

The 9th Duke of Devonshire used this key to formally open the new Queen Elizabeth's Grammar School building in The Green Road on 23 August 1909. The pupils processed through the town from the old building in Church Street on 12 November. In a very forward-looking move, girls were admitted for the first time, a total of 16 out of 71 pupils.

Earlier proposals to demolish the old Elizabethan school and redevelop the site were prevented by the intervention of the Derbyshire Archaeological Society in 1904. Plans for a new school were approved in January 1907 and the corner stone was laid on 23 September 1907. It was designed in 'Tudorbethan' style by County Council architect E M Longsden at a cost of £13,356.

Each year the key is now presented to the Head Boy and Head Girl as a symbol of their office.

L9
Portrait of Queen Elizabeth I

Copied c.1910 from 1580 original
Mrs G W Hall
Queen Elizabeth's Grammar School

After Queen Elizabeth's Grammar School moved to the new building in The Green Road in 1909, it was proposed to obtain a series of portraits of the original school founders of 1585. As none could be found, a portrait copy of Queen Elizabeth I was commissioned by George Edward Cokayne, a descendant of the principal founders, Sir Thomas Cokayne of Ashbourne Hall. A National Portrait Gallery copyist, Mrs G W Hall, carried out the work based on the 1580 original by Zuccharo hanging in the Gallery.

The painting was presented to the School on the 5 April 1911 and unveiled by Mrs Margaret Jelf, wife of Col. Richard Henry Jelf, CMG, DL, JP of Offcote.

Many large estates were broken up and sold in the 1920s, and country houses such as Calwich Abbey and Ilam Hall were completely or partially demolished in the 1930s. Ashbourne Hall survived in a much reduced state, but its grounds and deer park were acquired by the Urban District Council and completely redeveloped. In 1922 the original line of the road diverted in 1785 was partly restored by the opening of Cokayne Avenue. The first rentable council-built houses were constructed both here and at nearby sites. The main grounds leading down to the ornamental fishpond were laid out as the War Memorial Recreation Gardens and sports fields.

The technological advances in transport which had begun before the war now became paramount. Firstly bicycles and then motorised cycles, lorries and cars enabled workers to commute from the villages into the town or out of it to factories in Derby. Long distance motor lorries began to use the road from Manchester and Leek in the 1920s and 1930s, frequently failing to negotiate the bend at the foot of Swinscoe Hill and crashing through the parapet of Hanging Bridge. The introduction of motorised tractors on farms began to compensate for the wholesale slaughter of horses during the war, and steam-driven traction engines were used for harvesting and other tasks.

Ashbourne briefly had a steam-driven (omni)bus but it was soon replaced by vehicles powered by internal combustion engines. The Trent Motor Traction Company (now trentbarton) was founded in 1913 and operated its very first passenger 'bus' service between Ashbourne and Derby. Several village bus services provided local transport to and from the town and schools, notably Webster's of Hognaston (a firm whose history as carriers dated back at least to the 1690s). These allowed people from the villages to visit Ashbourne's two new cinemas – the Empire near the Station Hotel and the Elite in the Market Place.

Second World War 1939-45 and after

The Second World War saw many young men entering the armed services, but thankfully the town's casualties were only about thirty-five, far lower than in the first war. In 1941 an airfield was constructed on the 600-feet-high (183m) plateau immediately south-east of the town, approached from the Derby Road. Three runways and a permanent self-contained camp were laid out by some 3500 workers. A smaller satellite airfield was later built some four miles south on Darley Moor near Snelston. Both were intended as bases for heavy Wellington bombers, but due to the high altitude and unpredictable local weather they were relegated to a training role, flying Blenheim, Whitley, and Albemarle aircraft. Several crash landings occurred in bad weather, two of which took off the roofs of individual houses in Derby Road and North Avenue respectively. Haycocks, the clockmakers, were engaged in the war effort by making small metal pins and other items for Rolls-Royce in Derby.

After the war the large council Park Estate was begun on the former parkland of Ashbourne Hall south of the Henmore, and was followed elsewhere by extensive private building, particularly at the top of the old and new Derby Roads.

The ever-changing economic situation inevitably resulted in both losses and gains in terms of local employment. Both the textile mills near Mayfield survived by specializing, one in yarns and the other in tapes, webbing and narrow fabrics, but the corset factory closed and its site was redeveloped as a supermarket. The Nestlé dairy factory also closed when production was concentrated on its nearby plant at Tutbury, and part of its site became a small retail park. These losses have been partly balanced by new firms based on the expanding industrial estate on the old airfield, including a large new chicken processing plant. In addition employment for skilled engineers is now offered by three major international firms within a 15-mile radius – the Rolls-Royce aero engine factory at Derby, the Toyota car manufacturing plant at Burnaston, and the J C Bamford (JCB) excavator factory in and around Rocester.

The introduction of planning laws after the war helped to preserve the historic character of the town centre, which was designated as a conservation area containing no less than an hundred and sixty listed buildings, some of them in divided ownership and accounting for some two hundred properties. The conservation of the local countryside was enhanced by the creation of the Peak District as England's first National Park in 1951. Dovedale and most of the limestone country was included, and much also came under the protection of the National Trust. Tourism became a major source of income to the area and many farmers took advantage of this to offer accommodation or caravan sites. The greatly increased rise in car ownership also meant that more daytrippers visited the area, especially those bound for Dovedale or the Alton Towers leisure park.

This resulted in more traffic using both the narrow local lanes and the main through routes from Derby to Leek and Buxton. Heavy commercial vehicles increased in numbers, especially those transporting lime from quarries at Ballidon, Buxton and Brassington. These still have to negotiate the steep hill down into the town centre and pose safety issues to pedestrians as well as threatening the historic fabric of the listed buildings.

Some pressure was taken away from the town by the opening of the M6 and A50 roads which provided faster routes between London and Manchester, and especially by the Ashbourne southern bypass opened in 1994. This removed through traffic on the Leek route but there remains an urgent need for a northern bypass to serve the Buxton route.

As with most ancient market towns, the challenge to Ashbourne in the 2000s is to reinvent itself and to find future sustainable uses for the former houses and shops in the historic town centre. Numerous factors such as the increasing centralisation of public services, the growth of supermarkets, the globalisation of food and other commodities and the technological communications revolution have all reduced the importance of local services, shops and farming. The Urban and Rural District Councils were both merged with neighbouring authorities in 1974 to form the large West Derbyshire (now Derbyshire Dales) District Council, with its offices at Matlock. The railway line was closed to passengers in 1954, followed by total closure in 1963. Other locally based services such as the weekly cattle market and the magistrates' courts have disappeared, and whilst police, fire, and ambulance services still have a local presence they are largely operated from elsewhere.

The future appears to lie in providing specialist niche independent manufacturing and shops, quality outdoor leisure activities and accommodation for both foreign and UK visitors, and frequent popular cultural and heritage events. To achieve this the need to conserve and enhance both the rural landscape and the historic buildings and monuments which tell the story of the town's thousand year history remains crucial.

Select bibliography

The following select list of printed and manuscript documentary sources is arranged broadly by period, but many of the general sources also contain material for all or some periods.

Abbreviations
DAJ *followed by volume number and date* – *Derbyshire Archaeological Journal (all available online)*
DRS *followed by date* – *Derbyshire Record Society*
DRO – *Derbyshire Record Office, Matlock*

General sources
D Hey, *Derbyshire: a History,* 2008
Victoria County History: Derbyshire, 1905-07
Victoria County History: Staffordshire: Leek & the Moorlands, 1996
J Barnatt & K Smith, *The Peak District Landscapes through Time*, 2004
A E & E M Dodd, *Peakland Roads and Trackways,* 1980
C Hartwell, N Pevsner & E Williamson, *The Buildings of England*: Derbyshire, 2016
N Pevsner, *The Buildings of England*: Staffordshire, 1974
Rev J C Cox, *Notes on the Churches of Derbyshire, vol 1: Ashbourn,* 1875
K Cameron, *The Place Names of Derbyshire*, 1959
G Stroud, *Derbyshire Extensive Urban Survey Archaeological Assessment Report: Ashbourne*, 2001
Anon., *The History and Topography of Ashbourn,* 1839, reprinted 1978
Ashbourne Parish Registers, 1538-1919, & other church records, **DRO**
Ashbourne Old Trust records re grammar school and almshouses, etc, 1500s-1800s, **DRO**

Derby Mercury, Derbyshire Advertiser, & *Ashbourne Telegraph* newspapers*, 18th-20th C.*

Rev D and S Lysons, *Magna Britannica, Vol V, Derbyshire*, 1817

S Glover, *History of the County of Derbyshire, Part I Vol II*, 1833

R G Hughes and M Craven, *Clockmakers & Watchmakers of Derbyshire*, 1998

Prehistory & Roman

A Willis, *50 Finds from Nottinghamshire and Derbyshire,* 2016

T Bateman, *Ten Years Diggings in Celtic & Saxon Grave-hills,* 1861, reprinted 1978

C Hart, *The North Derbyshire Archaeological Survey to AD 1500,* 1981 (with extensive bibliography)

R Hodges, *Roystone Grange: 6000 Years of a Peakland Landscape,* 2006

J Collis, *Wigber Low, Derbyshire, a Bronze Age & Anglian Burial Site…*, 1983

J Barnatt, *Heritage Walks in the Peak District : Hartington–Alstonefield–Wetton ….,* 2006

G A Makepeace, & S M Elsdon, 'Recent Prehistoric and Romano-British material from Thorpe, near Ashbourne, Derbyshire', *DAJ 125,* 2005

G Guilbert, 'Artefacts from Thorpe Cloud.' *DAJ 115,* 1995

M Patterson, *Roman Derbyshire,* 2016

R W P Cockerton, 'The Development of the Roman Street system with special reference to Derbyshire', *DAJ 73*, 1953

A Henstock, 'The course of Hereward Street: a Reappraisal', *DAJ 100,* 1980

J Dool & R G Hughes, 'Two Roman pigs of lead from [Yeaveley] Derbyshire', *DAJ 96,* 1976

D J Breeze, *The First Souvenirs: Enamelled Vessels from Hadrian's Wall,* 2012 (including the Staffordshire Moorlands Pan)

Anglian

P Stafford, *The East Midlands in the Early Middle Ages*, 1985

M J Fowler, 'The Anglian Settlement of the Derbyshire and Staffordshire Peak District', *DAJ 74,* 1954

A Ozanne, 'The Peak Dwellers', *Mediaeval Archaeology vi-vii,* 1962-63

D Roffe, 'The origins of Derbyshire', *DAJ 106,* 1986

P Sidebottom, 'Ashbourne (St Oswald)', *Derbyshire and Staffordshire Volume of the Corpus of Anglo-Saxon Stone Sculpture.* Due to be published in 2017 by British Academy

Mediaeval

P Morgan, ed, *Domesday Book, 27: Derbyshire* (1978)

J Morris, ed, *Domesday Book, 24: Staffordshire* (1976)

D Roffe, *An Introduction to the Derbyshire Domesday Book,* 1990

S Jenkins, *England's Thousand Best Churches,* 2009

E A Sadler, *A Guide to Ashbourne (St Oswald's) Parish Church, Derbyshire,* 1934

G Shaw, G E & D H Buckley, *The Parish Church of St Oswald, Ashbourne,* 1991

Lincoln Record Society, *The Registrum Antiquissimum of the Cathedral Church of Lincoln 3,* 1935

Dean of Lincoln's valuation, 1329, Nottinghamshire Archives, DD.FJ 10/7/33

B E Coates, 'The Origin & Distribution of Markets & Fairs in Mediaeval Derbyshire', *DAJ* 85, 1965

G Turbutt, *The Hospitaller Order of St John of Jerusalem in Derbyshire History,* 1999

P Riden, 'The origin of the new market of Chesterfield', *DAJ 97*, 1977

Records Commissioners, *Rotuli Hundredorum 2,* 1812

Calendars of Inquisitions Post Mortem, (various dates)

Curia Regis Rolls, 1221-22, 10 *(Unauthorised market in Clifton)*

J R Maddicott, 'Robert de Ferrers, 6th Earl of Derby', *Oxford Dictionary of National Biography*

Earl of Lancaster's market lease, 1286, The National Archives, DL 29/891

Movement of archers in 1316-17, Nottinghamshire Archives DD 325/1

R Somerville, *History of the Duchy of Lancaster, 1265-1603*, 1953

I H Jeayes, *Descriptive Catalogue of Derbyshire Charters*, 1906

Rev J C Cox, 'Early deeds of Repton School', **DAJ 32,** 1910 *(Contains over 100 deeds all apparently relating to property on the de Mapleton family in Ashbourne & district in the 1200s and 1300s)*

A Saltman, ed, *The Cartulary [register of charters & deeds] of Tutbury Priory,* 1962

A Saltman, ed, *The Kniveton Leiger Book [register of charters & deeds],* **DRS,** 1977

J G Bellamy, 'The Coterel Gang an Anatomy of a Band of Fourteenth Century Criminals', *English Historical Review 79*, 1964

Royal Commission on Historical Manuscripts, *Report on the Manuscripts of Lord Middleton preserved at Wollaton Hall, Nottinghamshire,* 1911. *(Contains documents on the Coterel Gang)*

M Wiltshire, S Woore, B Crisp & B Rich, *Duffield Frith,* 2005

M Wiltshire & S Woore, *Mediaeval Parks of Derbyshire*, 2009

I Blanchard, 'Economic Change in Derbyshire in the Late Middle Ages, 1272-1540'; unpublished PhD thesis, London, 1967

E A Sadler, 'The ancient family of Cockayne and their monuments in Ashbourne Church', **DAJ 55,** 1934

R A C Cockayne, 'New thoughts on an old pedigree: a reconsideration of the Cockaynes of Ashbourne in the early fifteenth century and of their monuments in Ashbourne and Polesworth churches', **DAJ** *110,* 1990

E A Sadler, 'The family of Bradbourne and their monuments in Ashbourne Church', **DAJ** *57,* 1936

F C Eeles, 'Mediaeval triptych: remains discovered at Ashbourne Church', **DAJ** 65, 1944

C Hartwell, N Pevsner and E Williamson, *The Buildings of England: Derbyshire.* New Haven and London, Yale University Press, 2016

Tudor & Stuart

E M Yates, 'Map of Ashbourne, Derbyshire', ***DAJ** 80,* 1960

A Short, *The Development of Ashbourne Market Place in the 15th & 16th Centuries*, c. 2000

Lichfield Record Office: probate records, 1500s-1800s (various)

G Le Blanc Smith, *Haddon: the Manor, the Hall, its Lands & Traditions*, 1906

Records Commissioners, *Valor Ecclesiasticus, 1535,* 1810

M T Fortesque, *The History of Calwich Abbey*, c.1910

Rev J C Cox, 'Norbury Manor House and the troubles of the Fitzherberts', ***DAJ** 7,* 1885

E A Sadler, 'The earliest records of Ashbourne Grammar School', ***DAJ** 52,* 1931

N J Frangopulo, *The History of Queen Elizabeth's Grammar School, Ashbourne,* 1935

A Henstock, *Queen Elizabeth's Grammar School, Ashbourne, 1585-1985,* 1985

B Stone, *Derbyshire in the Civil War*, 1992

T Brighton, *Royalists and Roundheads in Derbyshire*, 1981

A Cockayne, 'The Life & Times of a Delinquent Cavalier: Sir Aston Cokayne, Catholic, Poet & Dramatist', *Derbyshire Miscellany 21/3*, 2017

E M Yates, 'Map of Ashbourne, Derbyshire' *Geographical Journal Vol CXXVI, 1960.*

H Nichols, M Wiltshire and S Woore, *A Catalogue of Local Map of Derbyshire c.1528-1800.* Llandybie, Dinefwr Press, 2012

Restoration

A Henstock, 'The Early Derbyshire Quakers and their Emigration to America', *Derbyshire Miscellany 8/1,* 1977

D G Edwards, ed, 'Derbyshire Hearth Tax Assessments, 1662-70', **DRS,** 1982

I Walton & C Cotton, *The Compleat Angler*, 1676

P Riden, P. 'Guest beds and stabling in Derbyshire, 1686-1756', **DAJ 128,** 2008

D Hey, Packmen, *Carriers & Packhorse Roads … in North Derbyshire..,* 2001

W R Holland, 'Notes on a measure of brass, dated AD 1677, and formerly in use at Ashbourne', **DAJ** 22, 1900

C Glover & P Riden, eds, 'William Woolley's History of Derbyshire', **DRS,** 1981

A Henstock, 'Cheese Manufacture and Marketing in Derbyshire and North Staffordshire, 1670-1870', **DAJ 89,** 1969

C N Dack, 'Urbanisation & the Middling Sorts in Derbyshire Market Towns: Ashbourne & Wirksworth, 1660—1830'; unpublished DPhil thesis, Leicester, 2010

C Henry, *English Civil War Artillery 1642-1645,* Botley, Osprey Publishing, 2005

Georgian

R Clark, ed, 'The Derbyshire Papist Returns of 1705-6', **DRS**, 1983

A Henstock, 'Ashbourne and the Jacobite Rising of 1745', in *Ashbourne and the '45*, 1995

B Stone, *Bonnie Prince Charlie and the Highland Army in Derby,* 2015

G E Shaw, *Matters of Life & Death* (Ashbourne Parish register extracts), 1990.

R Graves, *The Spiritual Quixote …,* 1773

A Henstock, ed, *A Georgian Country Town: Ashbourne 1725-1825*, vol 1, *Fashionable Society*, 1989

E A Sadler, 'The Mansion, Ashbourne.' **DAJ,** 53, 1932

E A Sadler, 'Dr Johnson's Ashbourne friends.' **DAJ** 60. 1939

A Henstock, ed, *A Georgian Country Town : Ashbourne 1725-1825*, vol 2 *Architecture*, 1991

T Brighton, *The Discovery of the Peak District*, 2004

A E & E M Dodd, 'The Old Road from Ashbourne to Leek', *Transactions of N Staffs Field Club, 83-84*, 1948-50

J B Harley et al, ed, 'Burdett's Map of Derbyshire, 1791', *Derbyshire Archaeological Society*, 1975

A D M Phillips, ed, 'Map of the County of Stafford by William Yates, 1775', *Staffs Record Society, 1984*

Rev J C Cox, *Calendar of the Records of the County of Derby*, 1899

E A Sadler, 'The French prisoners in Ashbourne.' **DAJ** *49- 50, 1927-28*

R Bennett, 'French Prisoners of War on Parole in Britain, 1803-14'; unpublished PhD thesis, London, 1967

G J Heldreich, *The History of the von Heldreich Family and their English Descendants*, 1990

S D Chapman, *The Early Factory Masters,* 1992

W Smethurst, *Notes on Ashbourne Clockmaking Families*, 1940

J A Robey, 'Samuel Harlow of Ashbourne and his Longcase Movements', *Antiquarian Horology*, March 2002

A Henstock, 'House Repopulation from the Land Tax Assessments [of Ashbourne] 1780-1820', *in* M Turner & D Mills, *Land & Property: the Land Tax, 1692-1832*, 1986

W Mottram, *The True Story of George Eliot*, 1905

E Welch, ed, 'Sion Chapel, Ashbourne: Letters and Papers 1801-17', **DRS**, 1998

R Emmerson, *Church Plate.* London, Church House Publishing, 1991

Victorian & Edwardian

A Henstock, ed, *Early Victorian Country Town: a Portrait of Ashbourne in the Mid-19th Century*, 1978

Directories of Derbyshire by *eg.* Pigot, Glover, Bagshaw, White, Kelly, etc, c.!822-1935

Tithe apportionments and maps, townships of Ashbourne, Clifton, Sturston, Offcote, 1846, **DRO**

Richard Cooper & Co., *Centenary History,* 1955

W Felkin, *History of the Machine-Wrought Hosiery and Lace Trades*, 1867

Rev G Smith, *Recollections of the late Francis Wright ...*, 1873

Rev S T Morse, *Archaeological and Graphic Illustrations of Ashbourne Church,* 1842

Ordnance Survey 25 inches to one mile, 1st ed. 1880, Ashbourne Sheet 43:2

Census enumerators' returns, townships of Ashbourne, Clifton, Sturston, Offcote, 30 March, 1851-1911

L Porter, *Ashbourne Royal Shrovetide Football: The Official History,* 1992

R Christiansen & J Miller, *The North Staffordshire Railway,* 1971

H Sprenger, *Rails to Ashbourne,* 2013

M Giddings, *Royal Air Force Ashbourne,* 1984

L Porter, *Victorian Times in and around Ashbourne: Photographs from the 19th Century*, 2000

L Porter, *The Spirit of Ashbourne: the 20th Century in Photographs*, 1999

H Hornby, *Uppies and Downies: The extraordinary football games of Britain.* Swindon, English Heritage, 2008

TIMELINE AND INDEX

Key:

National events
Local events
Ashbourne Treasures

1966	West German football team practice on playing fields
1970	River Henmore diverted under Shaw Croft
1985	Queen Elizabeth's visit to QEGS 400th anniversary
2000	Millennium clock erected
2001	Foot-and-mouth outbreak
2003	Prince Charles turns up Shrovetide ball
2005	Ashbourne becomes a Fairtrade town
2005	Development of Waterside Park starts (old Nestlé site)
2010	New St Oswald's Hospital opens
2012	New library opens

THE ASHBOURNE STORY

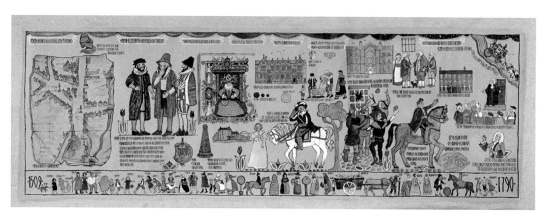